W9-BZL-698

THE EMBODIED SELF

SUNY Series in Philosophy
Edited by George R. Lucas, Jr.

THE EMBODIED SELF

*Friedrich Schleiermacher's Solution
to Kant's Problem
of the Empirical Self*

Thandeka

STATE UNIVERSITY OF NEW YORK PRESS

Published by
State University of New York Press, Albany

© 1995 State University of New York

All rights reserved

Printed in the United States of America

No part of this book may be used or reproduced
in any manner whatsoever without written permission.
No part of this book may be stored in a retrieval system
or transmitted in any form or by any means including
electronic, electrostatic, magnetic tape, mechanical,
photocopying, recording, or otherwise without the prior
permission in writing of the publisher.

For information, address State University of New York Press,
State University Plaza, Albany, N.Y., 12246

Production by Cathleen Collins
Marketing by Theresa Abad Swierzowski

Library of Congress Cataloging in Publication Data

Thandeka, 1946–
    The embodied self : Friedrich Schleiermacher's solution to Kant's
problem of the empirical self / Thandeka.
        p.   cm. — (SUNY series in philosophy)
    Includes bibliographical references and index.
    ISBN 0–7914–2575–4 (hc). — ISBN 0–7914–2576–2 (pb)
    1. Schleiermacher, Friedrich, 1768–1834—Contributions in
philosophical concept of the self.   2. Self (Philosophy)—
History—19th century.   3. Kant, Immanuel, 1724–1804—Contributions
in philosophical concept of the self.   I. Title.   II. Series.
B3098.S5T48   1995
126'.092—dc20   94–24788
                                                                        CIP

10 9 8 7 6 5 4 3 2 1

For Dean

Contents

Abbreviations

CPrR   Immanuel Kant, *Critique of Practical Reason*, Trans. by Lewis White Beck. New York: Macmillan Publishing Co., 1956.

D   *Dialektik*, aus Schleiermachers Handschriftlichem Nachlasse herausgegeben von Ludwig Jonas. *Friedrich Schleiermacher's sämmtliche Werke* III, 4, 2. Berlin: Georg Reimer, 1839.

S   *Grundlinien einer Kritik der bisherigen Sittenlehre. Friedrich Schleiermacher's sämmtliche Werke*, III, 1. Berlin: G. Reimer, 1846.

Preface

This book is a philosophic exploration of a dimension of the self that eludes common sense, cognition, and sense perception. I will use the philosophic work of the nineteenth century German theologian Friedrich Schleiermacher as a guide in this investigation, because he discovered a way to affirm the presence of a noncognizable, subject-less, object-less, life-infused self that I call "the embodied self." Schleiermacher described this self as the experiential ground of religious self-consciousness.

I am interested in this self for two reasons. First, I believe that as we approach a new millennium, we need to identify categories within our Western philosophic and theological traditions that affirm interconnection rather than isolation as a basic source of meaning and moral agency in our lives. An analysis of the noncognizable, embodied self delineated by Schleiermacher can help us locate and affirm these categories within our Western heritage. Second, Schleiermacher's use of categories that affirm the self as a part of the natural world allowed him to move beyond conceptual inadequacies that he found in the theories of the self developed by Kant, Fichte, and Hegel, among others. I believe that the philosophic and theological strategies Schleiermacher devised to overcome these inadequacies in the work of many of his contemporaries can help us construct our own strategies to move beyond inadequate theories of the self often found in postmodern celebrations of the disappearance of the self.

My goal in this book is to provide contemporary readers with a way to affirm unity rather than fragmentation, community rather than disruption, compassion rather than aggression as the sacred site of our humanity.

Acknowledgments

I would like to thank Kees W. Bolle, whose spirit of intense honesty and integrity brought me into the field of religious studies. I give heartfelt and grateful praise to Amos Funkenstein, who first introduced me to Kant and then insisted that I keep a focused gaze on the Kantian Problematic that Schleiermacher sought to resolve. I have special thanks for John B. Cobb, Jr., whose advice and encouragement in our correspondence and conversations helped me stay the course. I celebrate Jack C. Verheyden, who has my deepest gratitude, not only because he introduced me to Schleiermacher's *Dialektik* but also because he remained a sure, steady support and inspiring influence and guide during the many years I labored to bring this project to fruition. I am especially appreciative of Terrence N. Tice, whose careful reading of a draft of this manuscript provided me with a masterful array of subtle clarifications and suggestions concerning the German translations of Schleiermacher's work found in this book. The strength of this work owes so very much to these teachers and friends.

I take special pleasure in thanking my SUNY Series editor, George B. Lucas, Jr., whose ongoing belief in me and support for my project made this book a reality. I also wish to thank Mara Lynn Keller, my friend and former colleague in the Department of Philosophy at San Francisco State University, for devoting countless hours to reading and commenting on an early draft of this manuscript. The clarity of voice and style of this book owes much to her wise counsel. I am grateful to Anita Silvers, James Syfers and Nancy McDermid for the special academic leave time they granted me to work on this project during my four years at SFSU.

I had the good fortune to spend 1990–91 as a fellow at the Stanford Humanities Center while W. Bliss Carnochan was the director and Charles Junkerman was the associate director of the Center. That year and their support were crucial in giving me a collegial space of encouragement and goodwill needed to stay focused and centered on the research for this project.

The preparation of this manuscript, in its many stages of development, was guided by the wise and ever patient spirit and hand of Donna Chenail and the ongoing support of Peggy Bryant, Shirley Bushika and Lori Tolle of the Williams College Faculty Secretarial Office.

Finally, I would like to thank my partner, Dean Dresser, whose faith in me and unswerving commitment to this project helped get me through many long tormented nights of the soul.

Introduction

Friedrich Schleiermacher found the self that Immanuel Kant lost. An adequate account of this nineteenth century lost-and-found saga entails both historical reconstruction and philosophic reconsideration, and constitutes a little-known and poorly understood chapter in Kantian and post-Kantian studies. Such an account also has important consequences for contemporary thought, because it identifies and delineates a viable alternative to the "epoch of selfhood" that linked Kant, Fichte, and Schelling, and reached closure in the Hegelian system.[1]

The basic narrative line of the story recounted in the following pages can be readily summarized. Kant lost the embodied self, the self that is an inextricable part of the natural world, because of a gap in his critical philosophy. This gap is the absence of a necessary link between the noumenal and empirical self in Kant's theory of self-consciousness. Kant had made his theory of self-consciousness the foundation of his proof for the objective validity of the pure concepts of the understanding,[2] but he failed to demonstrate how pure self-consciousness (the 'I think') leads to knowledge of the self as an individuated, sentient, empirical being in particular, or to knowledge of the objective empirical world in general.[3] As a consequence, the impact of the noumenal self (pure thinking) on the world was rendered inexplicable in Kant's philosophy and the empirical self in its actual particularity became 'identityless', stripped of its historical content and gutted as a vital, living part of nature.[4] Simply stated, the self embedded in nature slipped through the gap in Kant's theory and lost its body. This is the self that Kant lost.

The legacy of this loss begins with Fichte. Fichte's original insight into the problematic structure of Kant's theory of self-

1

consciousness made "traversing of the gap" philosophy's new task.[5] Fichte established the post-Kantian 'entrypoint' for the retrieval of the self lost by Kant. Believing that Kant had not actually lost the empirical self but simply could not see it because his theory was inadequate for the task, Fichte tried to teach Kant's readers how to see the link between the pure self and the empirical self by means of a preconceptual standpoint called "intellectual intuition."

Hegel believed that he completed this task. Following Fichte's lead, Hegel affirmed intellectual intuition as the "absolute principle of philosophy,"[6] but unlike both Fichte and Kant, Hegel did not deem the realm of the suprasensuous to be beyond reason's grasp. For Hegel, reason became "the ultimate apex of nature's pyramid, its final product, the point of arrival at which it becomes complete."[7]

Schleiermacher, like Hegel, studied Fichte's early work. Unlike both Fichte and Hegel, however, Schleiermacher rejected intellectual intuition as the absolute principle of philosophy because he had discovered something that reason could not grasp: feeling [Gefühl]. Schleiermacher claimed that this non-sensate, nonemotional state of the self was the content of reason's nullpoint and as such was that which reason can never know. The gap in Kant's theory became, for Schleiermacher, feeling. Schleiermacher argued that the mind's eye could not see this gap (i.e., feeling) by means of intellectual intuition; rather, this precognitive feeling is a state of the self that is expressed in reason's cancellation. Schleiermacher identified the gap between the rational mind and the empirical world (which includes the rational mind's body) as the rupture in human consciousness that is felt. His philosophic task became that of justifying his claim that there is indeed a precognitive state of feeling of the self which intellection cannot know but which must nevertheless be affirmed. He recognized that in order to justify such a claim he would have to overcome "unconquerable difficulties." The story of Schleiermacher's retrieval of the self that Kant lost is in essence the story of the way in which he overcame these difficulties.

Schleiermacher's Critique of Modern Philosophy

The problem with modern philosophy, Schleiermacher argued, is that it has been given a predominantly religious character and is ridden with Christian principles in a totally inappropriate way. The basic error is that God has been thought of as a power modelled after our own forms of thinking (D422). Kant, for instance, attempted to ground the notion of God simply in the function of the will. Such a standpoint, Schleiermacher argued, pertains to reason, a human operation entailed in thinking (D428). Both Kant's practical philosophy and its Kantian modulation in Fichte suffer from the same basic problem: their one-sided reliance on thinking as an adequate means of expressing the transcendental ground of thinking. Schleiermacher believed that by such attempts to delineate 'knowledge' of God, metaphysical presumptions had become combined with the exigencies of the contingent (D377; D377n). He sought to break this metaphysical overlay on modern philosophy, which had reduced discourse to empty formulas and denigrated it to sophistry (D377). A distinction between philosophy and religious reflection had to be maintained (D436). At the same time, he sought to demonstrate that the same hidden unity lay at the ground of both philosophic reflection and religious experience. To achieve this end, he developed his *Dialektik* as a tool to ferret out thinking and reveal the nullpoint in its midst. This point of indifference, Schleiermacher argued, is not a gaping void but is full.

Schleiermacher believed that the incongruities in the work of Kant and Fichte were symbolic indications of the unrecognized and unacknowledged unity at the basis of all human experience. Each gap [*Spaltung*] was symbolic of the hidden unity that is the source of coherence and continuity in human experience. For Schleiermacher, this unacknowledged unity indicated flawed theories rather than the weaknesses of human faculties. Identifying himself as a man looking for the foundation of all philosophic structures, Schleiermacher actively sought to undermine Hegel's speculative system.[8] As Richard Crouter has suggested in his essay "Hegel and Schleiermacher at Berlin: A Many-Sided Debate," Schleiermacher not only anticipated but perhaps even precipitated the later nineteenth century revolt against Hegel's speculative system. Schleiermacher spurned the "imperialism" of Hegel's speculative philosophy and even played an active role in excluding Hegel from the Berlin Academy of Sciences. According to Crouter, "The exclusion of Hegel from this august group was no momentary affair; its effect was felt throughout his [Hegel's] career."[9] Schleiermacher believed that Kant (as well as Fichte and Hegel) had overlooked the fact that we are embodied *beings* who think. He sought to correct this oversight, believing that the failure to recognize, acknowledge, and understand the relationship of our being to our thinking resulted in the inability to ascertain the actual way in which we are aware of thinking's link to the world.

The first two chapters of this book serve as prolegomena to the delineation of Schleiermacher's discovery. We cannot understand Schleiermacher's solution if we do not first understand the problem and why it was so difficult to solve. Accordingly, these first two chapters constitute an introduction to the most basic problematic entailed in Kant's theory of the self. Gordon Michalson encapsulates this problematic in noting that Kant's critical philosophy tended to multiply "selves"—the "empirical" self, the "noumenal" self, the "transcendental ego"—rather than systematically show how they all finally relate to one another.[10] Schleiermacher, identifying the same problem more than 150 years ago, suggested that Kant was like someone who, when questioned about the fundamentals of a building, responded by pointing out the partitions that separate the rooms from one another (S20).

In chapter three I identify the way in which Schleiermacher made his discovery of the "common seed" at the core of Kant's theory of the self. In chapters four and five I will explicate and analyze Schleiermacher's actual discovery. In the interest of conciseness, I will not engage the considerable literature pertinent to various aspects of this account. Practically none comes even close to treating both the problem articulated here and its attempted resolution by Schleiermacher, in any case.

Schleiermacher's *Dialektik:* An Unfamiliar Story

Schleiermacher's recognition of and attempt to solve the problem of the gap in Kant's theory of the self was not unique. Johann August Eberhard, Schleiermacher's professor of philosophy at the University of Halle, sought to discover a means of filling in "the great gap."[11] I believe, however, that our ongoing failure to understand Schleiermacher's own solution to this problematic has resulted in the reduction of his insights to the confines of modernity and turned him into merely the progenitor and enigmatic father-figure of modern Protestant theology. This is ironic because as Emanuel Hirsch has rightly noted in his *Geschichte der neuern evangelischen Theologie*,[12] Schleiermacher established a doctrine of God on the basis of new fundamental principles.[13] Few theologians, Hirsch argues, have understood these principles. The Protestant world thus stands on the brink of a shift in consciousness that would render most of its thinking unfounded.[14] I have written this book to push us over the brink of this precipice, hoping that this movement beyond the confines of our flawed notions of God, self, and world will release us to a more inclusive and encompassing affirmation and celebration of life.

Schleiermacher's solution to the problem of the gap in Kant's theory of self-consciousness is found in his *Dialektik*, a posthumously published series of lectures delivered in Berlin between 1811 and 1831. These lectures have not been translated into English. For readers who have relied on English texts as their major source for Schleiermacher research, this is particularly problematic for two reasons. First, neither Schleiermacher's philosophy nor his theology can be adequately understood without reading his *Dialektik*. The core of both pertain to a prereligious and precognitive standpoint. Schleiermacher delineates the rules and procedures of this original mode of self-awareness only in his *Dialektik*.

I am in basic agreement with Hans-Richard Reuter's claim in his book *Die Einheit der Dialektik Friedrich Schleiermachers*[15] that no one can adequately interpret Schleiermacher's *Christian Faith* without having read and understood his *Dialektik*.[16] Paul Frederick Mehl reaches the same conclusion in his 1961 dissertation on *Schleiermacher's Mature Doctrine of God as Found in the Dialektik of 1822 and the Second Edition of The Christian Faith (1830–31)*.[17] Mehl skillfully demonstrates that the precognitive feeling that precedes the conscious feeling of absolute dependence on a transcendent ground (i.e., the conscious religious element in human experience) is not delineated in *Christian Faith*.[18] Mehl concludes that "on the basis of *Christian Faith* alone, it is hard to reply to Hegel's criticism" that the dog is the most religious being.

Mehl's analysis of the primary stage of religious consciousness found in Schleiermacher's *Dialektik* is insightful[19] but limited by two factors. First, it is restricted by his reliance on Odebrecht's reconstruction of Schleiermacher's *Dialektik*, which deals only with the 1822 lectures. Elsewhere in his lectures, Schleiermacher's discussion of this primary stage of religious consciousness adds further clarity to this stage. Second, Mehl's self-defined method of "internal analysis" leaves unattended much of the actual philosophic problem of modern philosophy that Schleiermacher sought to rectify.[20]

Mehl's choice of Odebrecht's text is understandable. As Mehl notes, the actual condition of the text of Schleiermacher's *Dialektik* has been a major hindrance to Schleiermacher-interpretation. Mehl characterizes the editions of the *Dialektik* by Jonas in 1839 and the subsequent edition by Halpern in 1903 as material bequeathed to us "in a strangely monstrous condition."[21] Neither Jonas nor Halpern attempted to reconstruct Schleiermacher's lectures into a completed, systematically disclosed work. Mehl agrees with Odebrecht that these lectures are the most important because in them Schleiermacher emphasizes the centrality of dialogue for the first time.

I agree with both Mehl and Odebrecht in their basic assessment of the importance of the 1822 series. Nevertheless, as this book demonstrates, I do not believe that an adequate understanding of Schleiermacher's highest standpoint can be provided solely by means of the lectures of this year. As a consequence, I have relied on the Jonas edition. Jonas, a student and close friend of Schleiermacher, was personally chosen by Schleiermacher to prepare his lecture notes for publication when he realized that his failing health would prevent him from completing the task.[22] Jonas used Schleiermacher's original lecture notes and various students' notebooks to prepare the text. The completed text consists of the six series of lectures that Schleiermacher delivered in Berlin in 1811, 1814, 1818, 1822, 1828, and 1831, and an introduction that Schleiermacher wrote for publication (*Beilage* F in the Jonas edition).

Jonas presents the 1814 lectures in their entirety as the "real [*wirkliche*] beginning of the *Dialektik*" (D viii–ix). Jonas also intersperses notes from different lecture series as footnotes to elucidate a given text. By so doing, Jonas demonstrates the basic structure and the overall coherence of the entire work. I am in agreement with Jonas's basic assessment of the underlying structure and coherence of the series of lectures. In working with the Jonas edition, I use texts from the entire series in order to present as subtle a rendering of Schleiermacher's highest standpoint as possible.

My choice to work with the Jonas text is of particular importance because the three major books in English on Schleiermacher's *Dialektik* have failed to grasp the primordial stage of Schleiermacher's delineation of religious experience. The three books are *The Philosophy of Schleiermacher: The Development of His Theory of Scientific and Religious Knowledge* by Richard B. Brandt;[23] *Schleiermacher's Experiment in Cultural Theology: The Eternal Covenant*, by Gerhard Spiegler;[24] and *God and World in Schleiermacher's Dialektik and Glaubenslehre: Criticism and the Methodology of Dogmatics*, by John E. Thiel.[25] This collective oversight constitutes the second problem for readers who rely on English texts for their primary knowledge of Schleiermacher. Each author misconstrues the central canon of Schleiermacher's *Dialektik*—that 'God' and the 'World' are distinct but inseparable ideas. They misconstrue this central canon because each fails to understand the way in which the gap in the theory of self-consciousness functions in Schleiermacher's work. Simply stated, each fails to understand the basic character of Schleiermacher's highest standpoint. In its stead, each author has posited his own peculiar standpoint, which leads each to an errant conclusion. Brandt claims that the canon entails a muddled and contradictory position on theism; Spiegler claims that the canon entails an incomplete and ruptured panentheist[26] position; Thiel simply finds the doctrine inexplicably muddled and refers back to Spiegler for clarification. I have written this book to correct this collective oversight in Schleiermacher interpretation.

Schleiermacher's solution has also been misunderstood because the problem in Kant's theory of the self has not been adequately grasped. As Kantian scholar Wolfgang Carl has demonstrated, the relationship between Kant's doctrine of the self and his deduction of the objective validity of the categories has not been adequately noted by most of Kant's interpreters. Carl demonstrates that Kant's doctrine of the self and the *subjective* deduction based on it were not understood by most of Kant's contemporaries, including Johann Schultz, whom Kant identified as the man who most understood his work as he intended it. Nor has this deduction, Carl continues, been understood by most contemporary Kantian scholars. They either misconstrue Kant's epistemic doctrine of self consciousness as pertaining to cognitive faculties (H. J. Paton), misplace it as the supposition of the Cartesian evidence of self-identity (Paul Guyer), or dismiss it as an unexorcised remnant of the misguided "psychological part" of Kant's *Critique of Pure Reason* (A. Riehl and P. F. Strawson).[27] Accordingly, my book situates itself in a highly contested area of Kantian scholarship.

Herman-J. de Vleeschauwer, in his groundbreaking three-volume work, *La Déduction Transcendentale dans L'Oeuvre de Kant*,[28] offers a vivid overview of the general problem of Kantian interpretation in which Kant's doctrine of the self is enmeshed. Vleeschauwer suggests that the inadequacy in Kantian interpretation can be explained, in part, by the positivistic standpoint of much of this scholarship. Vleeschauwer takes issue with the positivistic reduction of Kant's critical philosophy to a sole concern with the rules and principles of knowledge of the phenomenal world. He argues that Kant's discrediting of metaphysics was not absolute but provisional. In summarizing this problem, Vleeschauwer suggests that

The nineteenth-century fashion of allowing Cartesianism to take the place of the historical Descartes has been matched by a tendency to substitute the Critical philosophy and its later developments for the real historical Kant. Positivism found it advantageous to claim philosophical patronage for the scientific methodology which resulted in a limitation of knowledge to the realm of phenomena, and it was not unaware that the *Critique of Pure Reason* could be represented as its own justification avant la lettre. . . . On the other hand, if we look a little more closely, we see that a constructive effort [by Kant] accompanied the activity of destruction.[29]

Kant did not complete his task of reconstructing the self. Schleiermacher, I shall argue, completed this task in his *Dialektik.*

Schleiermacher did not discuss the content of the gap in self-consciousness in *Christian Faith*, his major theological treatise. This content, however, is the fundamental presupposition of *Christian Faith*. He referred to our immediate awareness of this gap in self-consciousness as immediate self-consciousness and expected the content of this state of the self to be self-evident for the reader of his dogmatics.[30] As suggested in paragraph 4,1, "no one will deny [the adequacy of his delineation of the two elements in temporal self-consciousness] who is capable of a little introspection and can find interest in the real subject of our present inquiries." His readers, he claimed, would find evidence to support his claim that "we never do exist except along with an other."

Schleiermacher had expected his readers to know through their own first-hand experience of introspection, the "common religious communion" accessible to all because it is based on "the absolutely common essence of humankind." Schleiermacher said as much in paragraphs 29 and 33 of *Christian Faith*.[31] Schleiermacher's assumption was premature. In defending himself against the barrage of charges leveled against him after the original publication of *Christian Faith* in 1821–22, Schleiermacher declared to his friend Friedrich Lücke that his critics had fashioned a Schleiermacher entirely unrecognizable to himself.[32] Faced with claims that his work was self-contradictory, reintroduced paganism, was perfectly compatible with the papal system of the Roman church, made faith in God inconsistent with his own position,[33] and that he himself was a gnostic, an Alexandrian, a proponent of monastic morality, a

Cyrenian, someone influenced by Schelling, by Jacobi,[34] and so forth, Schleiermacher declared that he was not whom his critics held him to be and in a high-handed manner urged them to first come to an agreement among themselves before turning their attention to him.[35]

The barrage of mutually exclusive and often conflicting claims about Schleiermacher's theology has persisted. As Ulrich Barth lucidly demonstrates in his survey of Schleiermacher-interpretation, scholars and theologians have concluded that Schleiermacher's link between self-consciousness and God-consciousness is basically adequate (Johann Friedrich Röhr); inadequate (Friedrich Wilhelm Gess); psychological (Christoph von Sigwart); pantheistic (Wilhelm Bender); ontological (Marlin E. Miller); a specific mode of time-consciousness (Hans-Richard Reuter); the basis for interpreting religion as mystical, anti-moral and anti-intellectual (Emil Brunner); philosophic ethics (Emanuel Hirsch); the basis for a system of aesthetics as the process of an ethical activity (Rudolf Odebrecht); inadequate as the basis for a philosophic doctrine of art (Edmund Husserl); platonic (Bernhard Todt); Kantian (Wilhelm Dilthey); Fichtean (Immanuel Hermann Fichte); Spinozistic and Schellingian (Christoph von Sigwart); and Jacobian (Eilert Herms).[36]

Schleiermacher, in fact, described his own *Dialektik* as a platonic method of inquiry (D371), a method that he considered to be constructive. Plato's dialectical method pertained to subjective intuition, an original mode of acquisition that first reduces the mind to the necessity of seeking knowledge, and then guides the mind into the way by which knowledge may be found.[37] This is the heart of Schleiermacher's own approach to his *Dialektik*. Schleiermacher described the twofold method of Plato's subjective intuition as follows.

> The first [step] is done by the mind's being brought to so distinct a consciousness of its own state of ignorance, that it is impossible it should willingly continue therein. The other is effected either by an enigma being woven out of contradictions, to which the only possible solution is to be found in the thought in view, and often several hints thrown out in a way apparently utterly foreign and accidental which can only be found and understood by one who does readily investigate with an activity of his own.[38]

Schleiermacher believed that the reader's contribution to the text through immediate self-disclosure was the missing link in

Plato's *Dialogues*. This missing link referred to the hidden unity that lies at the ground of all discourse and empirical knowledge. This hidden unity could be discovered only in the self. As Schleiermacher noted in his introduction to *Phaedrus*, "true philosophy does not commence with any particular point, but with a breathing of the whole."[39] Plato's *Dialogues*, which Schleiermacher characterized as works of art [*Kunstwerke*], pertained to the hidden unity that is the basis for all discourse and knowledge and as such, were not scientific exhibitions but methods of procedure (D444). Plato, according to Schleiermacher, knew that the rules of procedure and the principles for the construction of all knowledge were the same (D443).

Schleiermacher intended his *Dialektik* to exemplify a platonic art and science of discourse. He described his *Dialektik* as an art, because it sought the rules for the procedure in order to reveal something not at hand. It is also science because it pertains to principles and the coherence of all knowledge. Together, this art and science constitute the method Schleiermacher used to examine the nature and structure of conversation. Schleiermacher characterized his investigation as a study in speech, that is, the art of conversation. He defined conversation as two different but codeterminate series of operations of thinking [*Denkthätigkeiten*] that reciprocally refer to each other in the process of the mutual development (D569). Such activity can take place between two or more persons or within oneself. This activity also takes place when reading and writing entails thought (D371).

Conversation, for Schleiermacher, is the art of adaptable thought-development and thought-modification (D371). This means that if we think about something with regard to something else until we believe we actually know something and this is in fact actually the case, then we have arrived at knowledge through the art of conversation (D371). In other words, we have arrived at the completion of all possible alterations and developments of thought with regard to something. No more changes are possible. Thus there is absolute agreement that this something is the case. Accordingly, thinking and being (that is, that about which one thinks) are one.

Schleiermacher finds authorization for his idea of the coherence of thinking and being as the ground of knowledge in the fact that there is strife, that is, contested thinking. Strife, according to Schleiermacher, is disagreement about the relationship of thinking to being and is the surest proof of a basic coherency between our inner and outer reality. Strife indicates the active presupposition that thinking and being correspond. Even the most ardent skeptics are refuted by the very fact that they argue, since strife presupposes that there is something about which there is a disagreement (D584). Strife indicates that thought about a particular being, a 'something', is contested. That there is such a being is not contested. What is contested is its relationship to a given set of propositions. Schleiermacher wanted his *Dialektik* to establish the principles by means of which strife-free, or "pure" thinking (D600) can be established and the 'desire to know' [*Wollenwissen*] thereby led on to its goal. Accordingly, Schleiermacher envisions his *Dialektik* as the organon in this procedure for revealing the universal, timeless agreement and unity of all thinking and being (D603). This work is thus an examination of the movement of thought to knowledge.

According to Schleiermacher, the self is the original source of both identity and difference. Our 'first certain knowledge' is the oppositionality [*Entgegensezen*] of the *I* and the other. This is our first experience of difference, dissonance, and discontinuity. Our first experience of continuity [*Zusammenhang*], on the other hand, is that of the moments and functions of the *I* (D373). We are aware of our self-identity. The very possibility of thinking, that is, of discourse [*Gesprächführens*], is an account of this primal experience of identity and difference by the *I*. Schleiermacher intends his *Dialeklik* to be an account of this identity and difference; it is an account of the dividing and combining of thinking on its way to knowledge. The essence of this method is immediate self-disclosure.

Schleiermacher believed that Plato's chief goal was to bring the reader to this self-awareness. Plato's method necessitated the active participation of his readers. His written dialogistic form imitated the original and reciprocal communication between Plato and his followers.[40] Without the participation of the reader, nothing could be achieved; the reader must do the original work. Plato's goal was achieved when the reader was "driven to an inward and self-originating creation of the thought . . . , or [submitted] to surrender himself more decisively to the feeling of not having discovered or understood anything."[41] Accordingly, the "real subject matter" was "seldom verbally enunciated."[42] Rather, the reader supplied it by a subjective intuition. Schleiermacher had expected the readers of *Christian Faith* to have already experienced the hidden unity in self-consciousness for themselves before they turned to his theological text. Schleiermacher believed that this state of self-disclosure was the basis of all religious experience; *Christian Faith* began with this experience as a given. In contrast,

Schleiermacher did not expect the readers of his *Dialektik* to have already entered into this method of self-inquiry. Therefore, it is in the *Dialektik* that he provides a path, a deliberate methodology, for making this discovery.

Schleiermacher's Reconstruction of the Self

Schleiermacher believed in the integrity of human experience as a unity of thinking and being. He believed that our daily activity is based on our unstated presupposition that thinking and being correspond. Kant could not adequately explain this presupposition or our conviction concerning this theory of coherence because of the gap in his theory of the self. Schleiermacher wished to identify the source of this human conviction. To do this, he transformed the gap between pure and empirical knowledge into the source of the conviction within human beings that (1) we are whole and not fractured selves, and (2) the natural world is aligned with our inner process of knowing.

The strategy devised by Schleiermacher to solve this problem directly related to a platonic method of inquiry but with a nineteenth century post-Kantian Germanic spin to it: Schleiermacher delineated that which only the reader could provide—a transcendental standpoint of the self that would allow the self to see and feel the unity of thinking and being hidden by the gap between the noumenal and empirical self. In the work that follows, I shall argue that Schleiermacher's development of such a standpoint is Fichte's legacy to Schleiermacher.

Each person must peer into the gap and feel it. This is Schleiermacher's most basic claim. By so doing, each person will discover the actual nature of one's own unity and the source of the lived-conviction that our thoughts and the world cohere. Schleiermacher sought to "lure" us into this standpoint in his *Dialektik*. As such, his *Dialektik* is an attempt to construct a standpoint by means of which we can be immediately aware of the gap and its hidden ground of unity. For Schleiermacher, the gap was a prereligious, prephilosophic stage of human nature, which must be experienced in order to be resolved.[43] The fact that Schleiermacher believed that such an experience is possible can help us understand why his solution is so elusive (that is, we can finally understand it only if we have experienced it) and also why he believed that "every philosophy in fact leads the person who can see far enough, and wants to go far enough, to a mysticism."[44] Following Schleiermacher's lead, this present book thus becomes the narrative of the way in which each person can discover her or his own unity and integrity as a thinking self that is part of the organic world. This discovery will allow us to affirm a coherence that exceeds the grasp of reason. This was Schleiermacher's goal. The present work is my attempt to delineate the integrity of Schleiermacher's achievement.

Martin Redeker's characterization of the "pre-religious" center of Schleiermacher's religion serves as a useful introduction to the primordial stage of human consciousness.[45] Redeker notes that Schleiermacher

> himself referred to the center of his religion as mysticism. In romanticism the concept "mysticism" still had a broad and, one might say, "pre-religious" meaning. Mysticism seeks to exclude sense perceptions in order to partake of the more mysterious internal inspirations and intuitions. It means above all the sphere of intuition in which the epistemological division of subject from object has not yet occurred or has been deliberately avoided. In a pre-religious sense it could mean participation in the ultimate depths of life through existential encounter.[46]

Redeker believes that this pre-religious participation in the ultimate depths of life is the meaning of the mysticism that Schleiermacher applied to "the primal religious experience itself." For Schleiermacher, revelation was not a secondary experience acquired by learning or by adopting alien concepts. Rather, revelation was existential.[47] It "is experienced only in one's own existence."[48] This experience in one's own existence of the ultimate depths of life itself is the key to Schleiermacher's highest standpoint. This is the 'existential encounter' that lies at the core of Schleiermacher's life and work. In this book, I shall refer to this 'encounter' of self and world as one, as the initial stage of consciousness. This stage is the gap in self-consciousness because this stage is unknowable as an actual determinate moment of consciousness. At this stage, thinking is object-less and the self is subject-less. Schleiermacher's reconstruction of the self is the self that emerges from this immediate encounter with the fullness of life. The self that emerges is human nature certain of itself and celebratory of itself as an inextricable part of the nexus of the natural world.

CHAPTER ONE

Kant's Problem

Schleiermacher Discovers Kant

Schleiermacher's discovery of Kant was momentous. As Wilhelm Dilthey has suggested, "in Kant Schleiermacher learned how to think."[1] Schleiermacher first read Kant as a seminary student at the Brethren theological school in Barby, a Prussian town on the left bank of the Elbe not far from where it meets the Saal.[2] He had entered this Moravian seminary at age sixteen, in 1785, four years after the publication of Kant's first *Critique*, the *Critique of Pure Reason*. At Barby, Schleiermacher and two friends secretly read Kant's *Prolegomena to Any Future Metaphysics*, which had been published in 1783.[3] Schleiermacher later reported to his father that Kant had brought back "reason from the desert wastes of metaphysics into its true appointed sphere."[4]

If Kant did indeed teach Schleiermacher how to think, the Moravian Brethren certainly can be said to have taught him how to feel. The Moravian pietistic emphasis on personal religious experience rather than doctrine and dogma had first rekindled the spiritual heart of Schleiermacher's father, Gottlieb Schleiermacher, an Enlightenment theologian who served as a Reformed chaplain in the King of Prussia's army.[5] The father converted his wife, Katharina-Maria Stubenrauch, and their two sons Friedrich and Carl to the Brethren's faithfulness in Christ and then took his family to Gnadenfrei on April 5, 1783, to gain admission for his children into the Moravian schools. The family spent about eleven weeks in this community. During this period, Schleiermacher underwent his first

15

personal religious experience. He marked this experience as the birth date of his "higher life."[6] Concerning this experience, he would remark years later in a letter to his friend and publisher Georg Reimer that

> Here my awareness of our relation to a higher world began.
> . . . Here first developed that basic mystical tendency that saved me and supported me during all the storms of doubt. Then it only germinated, now it is full grown and I have again become a Moravian, only of a higher order.[7]

Schleiermacher's new spiritual awareness took root in the Moravian school in Niesky. Here, as Martin Redeker has suggested in his book *Schleiermacher: Life and Thought*, Schleiermacher became a Moravian outwardly and inwardly.[8] Schleiermacher was now enraptured by the devotion to Jesus characteristic of the Moravian life and he was enthralled by its communal life of worship, which entailed four daily services, monthly confessions, and monthly communion.[9] Schleiermacher also was given a strong humanistic education that included the study of Latin, Greek, English, mathematics, and botany. At Niesky, he and his classmates also had a great deal of time for private study. Here, Schleiermacher's mind and heart were given the grace to be one. This dramatically shifted when he transferred to the seminary at Barby.

At Barby, the unity between head and heart was sundered. Modern literature, philosophy, and all independent reading were forbidden. Schleiermacher, however, ate the forbidden fruit. Schleiermacher and his circle of friends, calling themselves "independent thinkers," smuggled in contemporary works such as Goethe's *Werther*. They also read Kant. Once discovered, they were severely disciplined.[10] Schleiermacher eventually persuaded his father to let him transfer to the nearby University of Halle. If he had not left voluntarily, he would most certainly have been cast out of this secluded Moravian garden by his theology teachers and advisers whom he now referred to as "the plodders."[11] Schleiermacher, at age eighteen, had become a child of the German Enlightenment. He was now highly critical of his professors' doctrinaire explanations, which seemed counter to reason. He confessed this to his father, in a letter dated January 21, 1787.

> I cannot believe [that Jesus] who named himself only the Son of Man was the eternal and true God; I cannot believe that his death was a substitutionary atonement, because he

never expressly said so himself, and because I cannot believe it was necessary. God, who has evidently created humankind not for perfection but only for the striving after perfection, cannot possibly wish to punish persons eternally because they have not become perfect.[12]

Schleiermacher's father replied,

O you foolish son, who has bewitched you, that you do not obey the truth? . . . Turn back! Oh my son, turn back![13]

Schleiermacher didn't. His father eventually recommended Kant's first *Critique* as well as the *Prolegomena* to his son to check his "fatal curiosity," lest he go astray in "the boundless desert of transcendental ideas without a safe guide."[14] Schleiermacher heeded his father's advice.

At Halle, Schleiermacher studied Kant with Johann August Eberhard, the university's most important teacher of philosophy.[15] Eberhard believed that Kant's critical philosophy was, at its best, Leibniz, and at its worst, dangerous in its presumptions about human nature.[16] Eberhard founded two journals, *Philosophisches Magazin* (1788) and *Philosophisches Archiv* (1791) to combat Kant's teaching.[17] Schleiermacher, who by now had read Kant's first *Critique* on his own, formed his own independent assessment.[18] Concerning this, Schleiermacher wrote to his lifelong friend Karl Gustav von Brinkmann that his "belief in this [Kant's] philosophy increases day by day, and this all the more, the more I compare it with that of Leibniz."[19]

Schleiermacher left Halle in 1787 and went to live with his uncle, Samuel Stubenrauch, an Enlightenment theologian who had taught at Halle and now had accepted a pastorate at Drossen, a country town not far from Frankfort on the Oder. At Drossen, Schleiermacher's father and uncle urged him to complete his studies and take his theology examinations.[20]

Schleiermacher eventually took and passed his exams but not before writing his first philosophic treatise, "On the Highest Good" (1789),[21] on Kant's second *Critique*, which had been published a year earlier, in 1788.[22] In this work, Schleiermacher criticized Kant for violating a principle of his own first *Critique*.[23] Kant, Schleiermacher argued, had enmeshed his moral philosophy in the dialectic of pure speculative reason by making the concepts *the highest good*, *God*, and *immortality* constitutive rather than merely regulative principles of human behavior; that is to say, he presented these concepts as the content rather than the forms or formal guidelines of moral behavior. By so doing, the goal of the moral cultivation and perfection of our will became not only possible but necessary. This part of Kant's moral philosophy, Schleiermacher concluded, at best is disjointed [*unzusammenhängend*]; at worst, it is incorrect [*unrichtig*].

Fourteen years later, in his *Outlines of a Critique of Ethics to the Present Time* (henceforth referred to as *Sittenlehre*),[24] Schleiermacher continued this critical assessment of Kant, now energetically dismantling the master's housing with his own tools. Someone doing a Kantian critique of Kant's second *Critique*, Schleiermacher argued, could very easily demonstrate the superfluous and faulty claim of Kant's use of the concepts freedom, immortality, and God in his ethics. Such a person would, with great justice, presume that such notions might have been produced upon speculative ground and therefore belong there (S22). Accordingly, for any critic who pays close attention to the structure of Kant's argument, Kant's building transforms itself into a child's game with vaporous [*luftigen*] building material [*Baustoff*], which is hit back and forth from one shore to the other.

Not once in Kant's theory, Schleiermacher argued, did one encounter a thought about a systematic tying together [*Verknüpfung*] of all human knowledge (S23). Rather than offering a systematic means of connecting the various sciences, Kant provides us with a description of that which keeps them apart (D20). Schleiermacher, in contrast, identified himself as a man looking for the foundation of all philosophic structures. To find this foundation, Schleiermacher believed that a standpoint higher than speculative reason was required. Kant's failure to be cognizant of such a 'higher standpoint', Schleiermacher concluded, made Kant's ethics a derivation of an idea, and precisely to this extent removed it as far from the theory of the soul as from that of the Supreme Being.

Schleiermacher, in his 1822 lectures on the *Dialektik*, argued that Kant (and Fichte) endeavored to ground transcendental consciousness sheerly on the agencies of human thinking (D428). Kant's work, Schleiermacher concluded, was incomplete because it was one-sided. Kant characterized human beings as coordinated acts of thinking without acknowledging that this coordinated activity takes place in our organic nature. Kant overlooked the fact that we are *beings* who think. The results were twofold: the failure either to ascertain the transcendent ground of being or to demonstrate that this ground of being is identical to that of the transcendent ground of thinking.

Schleiermacher sought to rectify this twofold oversight by Kant (and Fichte) in his *Dialektik*. This rectification entailed a redefinition of Kant's ethical subject. As Albert L. Blackwell has aptly pointed out in his book *Schleiermacher's Early Philosophy of Life*, Schleiermacher did not take issue with Kant in believing that there is such a thing as moral experience. Rather, given that we do indeed have this experience as an ethical subject, Schleiermacher differed with Kant as to how it is to be understood.[25]

Schleiermacher's separation of his own analysis of moral consciousness from that of Kant was precipitated by Kant's attempt to 'fill in' [*auszufüllen*] the place that he had emptied of speculative content. Kant then refurbished this room with the "practical data" of reason (Bxxi–xxii). The speculative ideas of immortality, freedom, and God gained credence in Kant's ethics by this process and it led Kant to his moral link to God. This is the link that Schleiermacher sought to challenge.

To understand the way in which Kant established this moral link to God, we now must turn to a discussion of Kant's second *Critique*, which is where Schleiermacher's formal criticism of Kant began. Here we find the roots of Schleiermacher's lifelong complaint against the "one-sidedness" of Kant's work. As we shall see, Schleiermacher believed that Kant, by relying on speculative reason to delineate moral consciousness, mistakenly filled in the place in knowledge he had originally cleared for faith. Schleiermacher believed that by so doing, Kant violated the principles of his own first *Critique*.

Kant's Moral Link to God

Kant, in his second *Critique*, transformed moral obligation into religious belief. This transformation made the link between practical reason and the will to action the ground of Kant's rational theology. According to Kant, in order to obey the precepts of moral law, we must believe in the objective reality of immortality, freedom, and God.

Kant summarized this process as follows. First, belief in immortality assures us that there is an adequate duration of time necessary for us to fulfill the precepts of the moral law. Second, belief in human freedom assures us that not only are we independent of the world of sense, but we also have the capacity to have our will determined entirely by the intelligible world. Third, belief in God is the necessary condition of this intelligible world that assures us of our obedience to moral law as the highest good by sanctioning this good by the highest independent good, that is, the existence of God (CPrR132).

Kant used the experience of the ethical subject as a source to establish the following link between practical reason and the will to action. In Kant's deduction of the principles of pure practical reason in his second *Critique*, he claimed that anyone who pays even the "least attention" to oneself will recognize the necessity and universal validity of the claim that moral law is given as an apodictically certain fact. Through self-attention, we discover that the moral law is "a fact absolutely inexplicable from any data of the world of sense or from the whole compass of the theoretical use of reason" (CPrR44).

Kant used this ethical subject to affirm that which he could not otherwise prove, that is, that moral law has its source in reason rather than the world of sense. This claim is self-evident, Kant argues, to anyone who pays attention to one's own moral consciousness. This consciousness reveals that moral obligation is not derived from sensate circumstance and, further, it also self-evidently affirms that our awareness of the law has impact on our will. According to Kant, through self-attention we discover that "the moral law ideally transfers us into a nature in which reason would bring forth the highest good were it accompanied by sufficient physical capacities; and it determines our will to impart to the sensuous world the form of a system of rational beings (CPrR43)."

Why are we "transported" by the demands of moral obligation? Why, as a being belonging both to the world of sense and the intelligible world (CPrR87), do we allow reason to rule the roost of our senses, emotions, and passions? Why do we pay tribute to this ruler in the form of a reverential respect that bows the human will to the legislation of moral law given to it by our own pure (practical) reason? What is entailed in the link between reason and will? Kant's answer is:

> Duty! Thou sublime and mighty name that does embrace nothing charming or insinuating but requirest submission and yet seekest not to move the will by threatening aught that would arouse natural aversion or terror, but only holdest forth a law which of itself finds entrance into the mind

and yet gains reluctant reverence (though not always obedience)—a law before which all inclinations are dumb even
though they secretly work against it. . . . (CPrR129)

What inclines our passions to become dumb in the face of the
sublime and mighty ruler named Duty? Kant's answer, at its most
basic level, is that the link between practical reason and the will to
action is the *engagement* experienced by a person in response to the
absolute, self-imposed demand of moral duty. This answer leads us
to the religious element in Kant's use of the ethical subject as the link
between reason and the will to action.

This religious element reveals the nature of the experience of
engagement that allows moral duty to hold sway over our passions.
This engagement is that of religious belief. We believe that 'Duty's'
commands are the commands of God. This belief is the core of
Kant's definition of religion. Writes Kant:

> Religion is the recognition of all duties as divine com-
> mands, not as sanctions, i.e., arbitrary and contingent ordi-
> nances of a foreign will, but as essential laws of any free
> will as such. Even as such, they must be regarded as com-
> mands of the Supreme Being because we can hope for the
> highest good (to strive for which is our duty under the
> moral law) only from a morally perfect (holy and benefi-
> cent) and omnipotent will and, therefore, we can hope to
> attain it only through harmony with this will. (CPrR129)

The link that makes possible reason's direction of the will is a
religious bond of engagement by the ethical subject. This link transforms moral awareness into religious belief. This transformation is
the transition that links practical reason and the human will.

I am in agreement with Emil L. Fackenheim's suggestion in his
essay "Immanuel Kant"[26] that the demand of absolute moral rectitude would have little affect if we experienced this demand in a disinterested way. We, however, are not disinterested but are engaged.
Our experience of the absolute demand of our moral duty is the
experience of engagement. Our *"engaged standpoint of finite moral
existence is metaphysically ultimate for the philosopher no less than for the
man in the street."*[27]

Caught in the crunch between our finite capacities and the
absolute demand, we are driven to the belief that the dualisms we
experience are not ultimate. This belief is expressed from our limited
finite moral standpoint as "symbolic anthropomorphisms."[28] The

terms in which this belief is expressed must not be understood
unequivocally, but only analogically. Simply stated, our notion of
God is a concept we are driven to as a way out of a moral conundrum. The idea expresses our radical inability to understand our
moral predicament, that is, that we, as finite moral agents, are
expected to achieve that which can only be expected of God.[29] As
Fackenheim suggests, Kant wants to prove that "belief in immortality and God is implicit in finite moral consciousness. He seeks to
develop, not philosophical concepts of God and immortality, but the
concepts of God and immortality which are implicit in finite moral
consciousness."[30] Fackenheim believes that if these "religious" beliefs
entailed in Kant's moral philosophy seem inadequate, the fault lies
not in Kant but in ourselves—in certain characteristics of our finite
moral consciousness.[31]

Schleiermacher, however, concluded that the unsatisfactory
nature of Kant's theory lay not in ourselves but in Kant. Kant's division of philosophy into theoretical and practical reason, Schleiermacher argued, exacerbated rather than solved the problem. This
division failed to identify the "common seed" out of which both theoretical reason and practical reason arise (S19). Kant failed to identify a transition by means of which the logical, the ethical, and the
physical aspects of human experience could be understood as inter-
related facts of human nature. To find such a transition, Schleiermacher concluded, a new paradigm for human nature must be
developed (S19–21).

Schleiermacher knew that our idea of God is a creation of our
finite standpoint as human beings. The idea of God, Schleiermacher
argues in his *Dialektik*, is always inadequate and entails contradic-
tions (D436). This, for Schleiermacher, was not the problem. Rather,
the problem he found with Kant's rational theology is that the *idea of
God* became associated with *that to which the idea refers* (D436). This
ongoing conflation of the two is unfortunate and has the appearance
of atheism (D436), he argued. Schleiermacher believed that "Kant's
polemic" against religion was a case in point of this conflation. The
"practical one-sidedness" of Kant's rational theology has its roots in
this misunderstanding (D436).

Schleiermacher strove to separate himself from this "appearance of atheism." To do so, he had to complete the errant unity
[*fehlenden Einheit*] of moral (religious) consciousness that Kant's
depiction of the experience of engagement of the ethical subject
entailed. In his *Sittenlehre*, Schleiermacher affirms that Kant is

indeed correct in seeking to establish a theology not founded on empirical knowledge. Rather, a "transcendental theology," the cornerstone in the foundation of all knowledge, is required (S23). But, Schleiermacher continues, let no one be deceived that Kant has actually discovered this foundation.

Schleiermacher believed that God is "ungiven." This ineffability, however, must not be confused with the 'God' of religious consciousness.[32] The idea 'God' and that to which it refers must not be confused. Schleiermacher strove to identify a higher standpoint in human nature that could maintain this distinction. To describe this standpoint, he had to redefine Kant's link between reason, the will to action, and the actual accomplishment of this action in the world. Kant had made the link the engaged self, the ethical subject. So, too, did Schleiermacher, but now the link between reason, will, and action was the engagement of the self that remains after thinking has been canceled. This engaged self is noncognizable because thinking has ceased. Using an insight from the work of Rudolf Odebrecht, we could say that Schleiermacher's assessment of religious engagement entailed the *coincidentia oppositorium* in which everything is put in the Nothing [*alles in das Nichts gestellt ist*].[33] This 'Nothing', as we shall see, refers to the nullpoint of thinking aligned to its noncognizable self. Schleiermacher's delineation of the human structure entailed in this 'Nothing' led him to the discovery of a rupture [*Spaltung*] in human consciousness that is the symbolic indication of the hidden ground of our unity as a cognitive and organic being (D435). Schleiermacher reached into this rupture and described what he felt, but only after overcoming seemingly "unconquerable difficulties."

In the second *Critique*, Kant suspended the domain of the senses as a determining factor in moral and religious self-definition, in order to render the human being a free agent. Thus Kant made the concept of freedom the

> keystone of the whole architecture of the system of pure reason and even of speculative reason. All other concepts (those of God and immortality) which, as mere ideas, are unsupported by anything in speculative reason now attach themselves to the concept of freedom and gain, with it and through it, stability and objective reality. (CPrR 3–4)

But what is actually entailed in the suspension of the sensible domain? What is the structure of this suspension? What formula is given to express this suspension so that it can be grasped in human consciousness? Finally, is such a complete suspension necessary in order to ensure the freedom of the human will, and thus, of moral agency?

Schleiermacher's Existential Link to 'God'

Schleiermacher believed that Kant's suspension of the sensible domain in order to make room for faith had failed to answer these questions. Kant's formulation for belief in God was therefore incomplete. Accordingly, Schleiermacher sought to develop his own answers to these questions in his *Dialektik* by suspending thinking in order to discover what, from the standpoint of the human being as part of the natural world, is suspended in sentient being. Wanting to find in the self as an organic agent of the world, the counterpart to that which propels one into faith, Schleiermacher acknowledged that this task presented him with "unconquerable difficulties" so long as he began with thinking and its thoughts (D423). How can thinking formulate that which it cannot think? Obviously, it cannot. Schleiermacher's quest would thereby have reached its end if human beings were simply the being of thinking, or the Cartesian *cogito*. Human beings, however, are more than this. Simply stated, Descartes had made a basic mistake in his formulation of the thinking subject.

According to Schleiermacher, the meaning of Descartes's proposition *Cogito, ergo sum* is that the subject, with regard to thinking, is identical in all of the alterations of its individual moments of thinking (D529). The basic problem with this formulation is that so long as a different form of activity by the subject is not taken into account, there is no basis for the subject to think of its moments of thinking as differing one from the other. Without this *difference*, there is no way in which the identity of the subject can be affirmed [*behaupten*].

By contrast, Schleiermacher does not allow this separation of thinking and being to stand as a basis for self-consciousness. Rather, self-consciousness becomes, in Schleiermacher's work, the identity of the two (D529). Our being is not simply an expression of thinking; we are also the being that does the thinking. Our thinking, according to Schleiermacher, is an expression of our organic nature (D528n). The self, from this standpoint, is an organic agent that generates thought. Our being is the power of life in existence. Thinking is an expression of this power. The two, however, are not the same.

Kant, as we have seen, elevated 'man' "above himself as a part of the world of sense" (CPrR 86). But Kant also knew that reason stretches its wings in vain when it attempts to soar above the world of sense by the mere power of speculation (A591; B619). Schleiermacher wished to bring man back to his senses.

An entry in Schleiermacher's journal in 1800 serves as graphic illustration of his intention to reunite the mind with its body. Here, he wrote that "The human being is an ellipse; one focus is the brain and the other the genitals."[34] This entry is in keeping with the bodily imagery found in his *On Religion*, first published in 1799.[35]

In the first edition of *On Religion*, Schleiermacher uses the imagery of the body's sense organs and the metaphor of the bridal embrace to illustrate the original unity of mind and body, subject and object, thinking and being, percept and perceiver, which religious experience presupposes.

In describing the "first mysterious moment" in sense perception in which sense organ and its object "have so to speak, become one and have flowered into one another—before both return to their original place," Schleiermacher's description of this "indescribable" and "fleeting" moment deserves to be cited at length. Concerning this original unity, Schleiermacher writes:

> It is as fleeting and transparent as the first scent with which the dew gently caresses the waking flowers, as modest and delicate as a maiden's kiss, as holy and fruitful as a nuptial embrace; indeed, not *like* these, but it *is itself* all of these. A manifestation, an event develops quickly and magically into an image of the universe. Even as the beloved and ever-sought-for form fashions itself, my soul flees toward it; I embrace it, not as a shadow, but as the holy essence itself. I lie on the bosom of the infinite world. At this moment I am its soul, for I feel all its powers and its infinite life as my own; at this moment it is my body, for I penetrate its muscles and its limbs as my own, and its innermost nerves move according to my sense and my presentiment as my own. With the slightest trembling the holy embrace is dispersed, and now for the first time the intuition stands before me as a separate form; I survey it, and it mirrors itself in my open soul like the image of the vanishing beloved in the awakened eye of a youth; now for the first

time the feeling works its way up from inside and diffuses itself like the blush of shame and desire on his cheek. This moment is the highest flowering of religion. If I could create it in you, I would be a god; may holy fate only forgive me that I have had to disclose more than the Eleusinian mysteries.

This is the natal hour of everything living in religion. But the same thing happens with it as with the first consciousness of human beings that retires into the darkness of an original and eternal creation and leaves behind for us only what it has produced. I can only make present to you the intuitions and feelings that develop out of such moments.[36]

This is a far cry from the "sublime and mighty, moral duty" imagined by Kant, "that doeth embrace nothing charming or insinuating but requirest submission" (CPrR86).

In 1831, three years before his death, the mature Schleiermacher spoke with the restrained language of an elder statesman. Nevertheless, he reaffirmed his youthful affirmation of the unity of mind and body, by stating that "self-consciousness is consciousness of life" (D529). In self-consciousness, we are conscious of our own being and regard our being as part of the totality of being (D517n). This immediate awareness of being is not an abstraction. It is not a speculative awareness of the universal form of being (D529). It is not an awareness induced by the mind abstracted from life. That awareness is not the presence of life itself. That abstraction pertains to knowledge in and of itself, but not to the immediate experience of life.

In the third edition of *On Religion*, the mature Schleiermacher revised the passage cited above, but continued to affirm the importance of the unity of body and mind in "every religious stirring." Concerning this moment of unity, Schleiermacher now wrote:

It is the holy wedlock of the universe with incarnate reason, direct, superseding all error and misunderstanding, consummated in a creative embrace. When this happens to you, you lie, as it were, on the bosom of the infinite world. In that instant you are its soul, because you feel, if only through one part of you, all its powers and its unending life as your very own; it is your body, because you penetrate its muscles and members as if they were your own, and our senses and expectations set its inmost nerves in motion. This is how the initial conception of every vital and original moment of your life is made. This is how each new moment comes to belong within your life's domain. Out of such a beginning, moreover, arises every religious stirring.[37]

Schleiermacher sought a formula for self-consciousness that pertained to the presence of actual, organic life. This immediate presence of organic life was not taken into account in Kant's rational theology. (Gordon Michalson's claim that "Kant's deep suspicion of our bodies" helps account for Kant's explanation of the universality of radical evil certainly is sound.[38]) As we can see in the quotes above, Schleiermacher, in stark contrast to Kant, celebrated the body as part of the human link to God.

As was suggested at the beginning of this chapter, Kant taught Schleiermacher how to think. Schleiermacher subsequently turned his enlightened, critically trained mind to the master's own work and found it one-sided. To rectify this imbalance, Schleiermacher had to devise a way of talking about the noncognizable self of human experience. Schleiermacher knew that this organic agency of the self is the site of the gap in Kant's critical philosophy. His task was to devise a new vocabulary that would allow him to grasp this self. To understand Schleiermacher's new lexicon, we must first understand the language he had to overcome. Kant's language, as we shall now see, prevented him from knowing that the organic self—the embodied self—was missing in his critical philosophy. Our discussion now turns to Kant's discovery of the gap in his work and the aporia in Kant's first *Critique* that kept this discovery so long from view.

Kant Discovers the Gap in His Critical Philosophy

In 1798, ten years after the publication of his second *Critique* and seventeen years after the publication of his first *Critique*, Kant came face to face with the gap in his critical system.[39] He realized that he had failed to disclose a necessary connection between the self's inner world and outer world. He had not established a necessary transition between the way in which the self thinks about nature as an a priori science (that is, metaphysics) and the way in which the various processes of nature empirically disclose themselves to us (that is, physics).[40] Bereft of this link to the world, the self lost its connection to its own body as part of the empirical world.

Eckart Förster has traced the way in which Kant discovered the gap in his critical philosophy. Kant's discovery, Förster argues, is directly related to the function Kant assigned to the *Metaphysical Foundations of Natural Science* in his critical philosophy.[41] In the *Metaphysical Foundations*, Kant delineated the principles of external intuition in their entirety in order to prevent his *Critique* from "groping among meaningless concepts."[42]

Kant intended his *Metaphysical Foundations* to demonstrate that the categories and principles of the understanding have real applicability and objective reality. Förster contends that this intended use by Kant of his *Metaphysical Foundations* can be adequately understood only if it is placed within the context of a shift that took place between the first and second editions of his first *Critique*.[43]

In the first edition, Kant wished to demonstrate the objective validity of the pure categories of rational thought. According to Kant, these pure categories pertain only to appearances, to phenomena, not to noumena. Without this restriction to the phenomenal realm, Kant claims, "all meaning, that is, relation to the object, falls away" (A241). Transcendental philosophy specified not only the rule that is given in the pure concept of the understanding but could "also specify a priori the instance to which the rule is to be applied" (A135). In his first edition, Kant specified this a priori instance by means of *inner* intuition (in the Schematism chapter).

In the second edition, "a subtle shift" in Kant's position took place.[44] Kant now specified precisely which intuitions concerned him—*outer* intuitions. Henceforth, he must show that his transcendental principles apply a priori to instances of external, corporeal nature, that is, to empirical bodies. Accordingly, Kant now required the form and principles of *external* intuition—a general doctrine of body (B288–91). Without outer intuitions, Kant now argued in his *Critique*, metaphysics "gropes, uncertain and trembling among mere meaningless concepts." Kant intended his *Metaphysical Foundations* to delineate this general doctrine of body to which the transcendental principles of his critical philosophy apply a priori. Thus, in 1798, when Kant realized that his *Metaphysical Foundations* had not fulfilled its assigned role in his critical philosophy, a gap "suddenly" appeared before him.[45] Kant now realized that he had not yet demonstrated a necessary bond between the a priori principles of understanding and the external objects to which they apply. The ground of his claim that the 'I think' is a perception, or an indeterminate empirical intuition, had not yet been demonstrated (B424). Simply stated, Kant now realized that he had lost the self's body.

Kant had lost the self's body by not explaining how the 'I think' can be an empirical proposition even though the 'I' in this proposition is not an empirical representation but is purely intellectual (B423). He had not demonstrated the interconnection between the thinking-self and the self as a corporeal being. As Förster notes, the question that now arose for Kant was how does the I "proceed from the 'I think' and determine the given manifold in such a way as to yield empirical knowledge of myself as an existing, corporeal being in space and time."[46]

Kant's answer was the ether, which he conceived of as the collective totality of all possible experiences. He wanted to delineate an a priori system of corporeal nature, that is, the moving forces of matter, as a further elaboration of the "material" supplied to thought.[47] As Kant had suggested in his first *Critique*, experience is impossible without material (B430). Without this material, Kant believed that the *actus* 'I think' would not take place (B423). Kant was now confident that his present work on the ether would fill in the gap between thinking mind and physical body, and thereby complete "the task of the critical philosophy."[48]

The ether might also be conceived of as the self in Kant's system. The self, Kant claimed, is at one and the same time both subject and object in respect of existence, in so far as the proposition 'I think' asserts 'I exist thinking' (B429). In other words, the self as *subject* is that which is aware of its existence, and the self as *object* is that of which the subject is aware. The collective totality of the self as object is therefore the very possibility of all of the subject's experience. This collective totality of the self coincides with Kant's description of the ether as the object of thought, the dynamic continuum of the agitating forces of matter.

The self as its own object became an object constituted by moving forces. Kant now attempted to discover the agitating forces of matter within the self that are the ground for the self's awareness of exterior matter. Not surprisingly, Kant wavered in the way in which he thought of the extensive continuum of matter known a priori by the self. This continuum is the "stuff" of thought but is it mental or physical? Both perspectives are implicit in Kant's position.[49] Förster believes that Kant finally affirmed that the ether was an ideal of reason. The ether was the way in which the mind must think about things.[50]

Burkhard Tuschling, on the other hand, in his essay "Apperception and Ether: On the Idea of a Transcendental Deduction of Matter in Kant's *Opus postumum*"[51] disagrees with Förster's conclusion. Tuschling believes that Kant's new principle blurred the distinction between mind and matter, and that this led to an "absolute idealism." Tuschling believes that primary matter is at the root of Kant's new deduction. All experience is united in an absolute totality, that is, in the concept of an object. This object is now the only object of possible experience. From Tuschling's perspective, Kant attempted to establish, a priori, "the absolute totality of the synthetic unity of perception," or "the material principle of the unity of possible experience"[52]

Kant sought to demonstrate how this totality could be deduced from the self because the self as its own object is the collective totality of material without which experience would be impossible.[53] The object of understanding was no longer a posteriori but a priori to empirical, sensible data. According to Tuschling, "the borderlines between intuition, concept of the understanding, and concept of reason, or, respectively, between Aesthetic, Analytic, and Dialectic [were blurred]."

Tuschling concluded that Kant, in taking this step, never made it to the other side of the gap.[54] He never found the "missing link" between apperception and the ether. Kant had wanted to maintain his realist postulate, but he could not rectify the standpoint of his absolute idealism with his claim that there is indeed a world ontologically distinct from us but nevertheless necessarily aligned to our pure categories of thought.

Förster disagrees with Tuschling's conclusion and argues that Kant wavered. Förster believes, however, that Kant finally reaffirmed the basic tenets of his critical system by making the unique object of experience an ideal.[55]

I shall not attempt to arbitrate this dispute between Förster and Tuschling. Rather, I follow the lead of Jules Vuillemin, who, in his formal response to both positions, set aside these differences as merely technical in the light of a far "more questionable" assumption by Kant in his theoretical deduction.[56] Kant assumed that the concept—"the very possibility of experience"—has meaning. This concept, Vuillemin suggests, "is probably the most elusive concept in transcendental philosophy."[57] It is elusive, Vuillemin suggested, because it is illusionary: "Kant's struggle . . . was a struggle after a chimera."

Vuillemin's criticism questions the very heart of Kant's Copernican revolution. Kant sought to determine an a priori condition of the self that makes determinate experience possible. This is the purpose of his transcendental deduction in the first *Critique*. Kant's critical philosophy is not solely concerned with the rules and principles of knowledge of the phenomenal world. He believed that the foundation of knowledge must be sought within the self. He also believed that this foundation was not something subjective, which is simply linked to the inner state of the individual subject. Rather, this experience pertains to consciousness in general. Kant referred to this state as transcendental apperception in 1781 but retreated from this term because of the charge of idealism. Experience, however, subsequently presupposed for Kant "the sensible percept outside the individual and subjective frame of the subject of perception and this gave to it its character of objectivity and its own validity."[58] This is the heart of Kant's realist postulate, which he never purposely sought to abandon.

Schleiermacher never challenged Kant's realist postulate. Nor did Schleiermacher question the legitimacy of establishing the unity of the self as the link between thinking mind and organic matter. Schleiermacher simply questioned the soundness of Kant's own explanation of this link. Wilhelm Dilthey believes that Kant's influence on Schleiermacher's *Dialektik* rests upon the fundamental Kantian idea of the link between our (inner) concepts and the (outer) world. Kant, Dilthey argues, demonstrated that there is no metaphysics exceeding the world of experience of science. Rather, "where any actual thinking is, it is there linked with the matter [*Materie*] of our experience."[59] It is this link that led Schleiermacher to proclaim that Kant had brought "back reason from the desert wastes of metaphysics into its true appointed sphere."[60]

Kant's a priori Aporia:
The Two Selves in Kant's First *Critique*

The gap in Kant's system could be kept from view by a basic equivocation in Kant's first *Critique*: Kant's doctrine of the self was ambiguous—or to use Michalson's term, it "wobbled."[61] The same term [*Selbst*] referred both to thinking as an original, spontaneous *act* (B130) and to self-consciousness as the 'I think', the *representation* of this spontaneous act (B132).

The original act is unmeditated and generative. It generates thought and is that which is required if we are to attain consciousness. In other words, if thinking about something entails the production of mental representations, we must first have the very capacity to generate these representations. This capacity is the actual generating of representations. This generating activity is thinking, which is an original, spontaneous act of understanding.

Kant called this fundamental human capacity to generate thought so as to be able to think about things the "faculty of understanding" (B130). The spontaneous act to which Kant referred in Proposition fifteen of his "Transcendental Deduction of the Pure Concepts of the Understanding" is thus not a determinate or determinable thing, but rather an act—an act of understanding. It is that which makes our awareness of things possible. This spontaneous act of understanding is the first referent for the *I* in Kant's theory of the self. This self is the pure, unmediated activity of thinking. Here, there is no distinction between subject and object; the one *is* the other. This act of generating thought is preconscious.

The representation of this act, on the other hand, refers to a conscious self rather than to a preconscious activity of the self. According to Kant, the original spontaneous act of understanding generates the representation 'I think'. This 'I think' representation is "empty" of sensible content (B132). Kant refers to this representation as the first and original consciousness of the subject. This consciousness is self-consciousness, the awareness of the self as thinking in general. This is what Kant means by the term pure or original apperception.[62] The subject self is aware of itself as its own object. This thinking is first and foremost thinking about itself.

As stated above, Kant's first self is an original act, the second is a derivative of this original act. The second is generated by the original act and as such is a product of the original act. The first self refers to thinking in general. The second refers to (possible) consciousness of thinking, that is, to self-consciousness. This second self is actual deliberation [*Überlegung*], which Kant identifies as reflection (reflexio). It is deliberate thinking about thinking. It is consciousness of thinking as the awareness of thinking's relationship to itself. It is reflection on the *relationship* of thinking to the thinking entailed in thinking about something.

Dieter Henrich, in his essay "Kant's Notion of a Deduction," uses transcripts of Kant's lectures to clarify Kant's theory of reflection. Henrich divides Kant's theory into four steps,[63] which can be summarized as follows: (1) Our cognitive capacities entail numerous operations; they are a "mingled web." (2) Each of these capacities has its own domain and is spontaneous in its operation. (3) These operations must be controlled and stabilized so as to keep them in the limits of their proper domain. This controlling and stabilizing process is the activity of reflection. Writes Henrich, "Without [reflection] we would, for example, confuse counting with calculating, analysis with composition, and so forth. Kant says explicitly that without reflection we would only utter meaningless sequences of words."[64] (4) Reflection is therefore our spontaneous awareness of our cognitive activities and of the principles and rules upon which they depend. Reflection, as such, is the precondition of rationality.

Reflection, accordingly, is not something that is achieved by conscious, deliberate philosophic investigation. Rather, it is the source of philosophic insight. The original unity of apperception is this process of "reflected control."[65] It is neither a concept nor a sensible intuition and is prior to all theorizing. This original unity of apperception has two tasks. First, it accompanies any reflectively accessible knowledge. Second, it is the origin of the system of the categories and the point of departure for the deduction of the legitimacy of their usage. The system of the categories implies that "reflection is omnipresent because reason is one."[66] According to Henrich, "The unity of reason, as far as the systematic structure of its principles is concerned, is represented in the most fundamental way by the implications of the thought "I think," the system of the categories."[67]

The unity of reason, as Henrich rightly notes, is implied. It is not immediately given. As such, Henrich's explanation does not resolve the problem of the two selves in Kant's theory of the self. Neither Henrich's explanation of Kant's theory of reflection (and concomitantly of the unity of apperception) nor Kant himself makes adequate note of the distinction between the unity of reason and the reflection process that accompanies knowledge of it and is in fact the source of our knowledge of it.

Henrich concludes that Kant's theory is "conceived and designed in a perfectly consistent way."[68] Henrich, like Kant, has failed to adequately explain how the distinction between the actual activity of reason unifying itself, and the 'I think', which is the representation that *implies* this unifying activity in consciousness, is achieved. As Henrich rightly notes in his essay, "Fichte's Original Insight," Kant, like Descartes and Leibniz, did not think it philosophy's purpose to examine the structure of self-consciousness. Exploration of the self was not deemed to be philosophy's task.[69] Self-consciousness simply played the role of a "grounding-principle."[70] Accordingly, the ground of this grounding principle remained in the shadows.

Herman-J. de Vleeschauwer suggests in the third volume of *La Deduction Transcendentale dans L'Oeuvre de Kant*[71] that this gap was initially kept from view by Kant's equivocal use of the term 'the synthetic unity of apperception'. "In synthesis," Vleeschauwer states, "the whole mystery of the mechanism of objectification is to be found."[72] But Kant leaves this mechanism in the dark. True synthesis, Vleeschauwer argues, is an act. It is a doing. It is a function. The synthetic unity of consciousness in Kant, on the other hand, is the form in which we are aware of the act. Kant, by making the act a presupposition of consciousness, treats this 'doing' as something that is done (in consciousness).[73] The synthetic unity of consciousness thus becomes both: the awareness of the act and the final referent for the act itself. The difference between the actual act and the awareness of the act is obscured by making the synthetic unity of consciousness the final reference for both. This difference obscured, the structure of their identity remains hidden. The 'wobbling' in Kant's theory of the self had received its final scaffold.

The imprecision in Kant's principle with regard to the identity and difference of the act and the form in which it is known results in an inadequate demarcation of the differences between synthetic unity, the analytic unity of judgment, and the actual act of synthesis. This imprecision and ambiguity can be traced back to the equivocal nature of Kant's theory of self, which, when all is said and done, is his highest epistemological reference.[74] Because the unity of the self in Kant's theory is never firmly established, the foundation upon which his entire philosophy rests remains unclear. Vleeschauwer suggests that we have only to remove the complex and intricate scaffolding of Kant's critical theory in order to discover that virtually nothing has been explained.[75]

The gap in Kant's theory, once discovered, loomed too large to be ignored—even by Kant. Fichte, Schelling, and Hegel sought to solve the problem. So, too, did Schleiermacher. Schleiermacher dismissed Fichte's solution. He also rejected Schelling's and Hegel's solutions. Schleiermacher believed that none of these solutions actually retrieved the body that Kant had lost because of the one-sidedness of the idealism that each propounded.

Idealism's One-sidedness

Schleiermacher considered Fichte and Schelling the chief proponents of the two major schools in German Idealism of his generation.[76] Schleiermacher shared with Fichte and Schelling the Kantian-inspired goal of a philosophically demonstrated transcendent ground of all knowledge situated in the unity of the self. But he spurned the "one-sidedness" of both their philosophies.

Schleiermacher rejected Fichte's assertion of the absolute incompatibility of idealism and realism. Fichte claimed that idealism and realism could not be reconciled.[77] In the *Dialektik*, Schleiermacher sought to demonstrate the common ground of these two philosophic systems. To do this, he argued that freedom and necessity, like intellect and matter, are polar perspectives of the same empirical experience. Fichte's failure to understand this, Schleiermacher concluded, made his philosophy "one-sided" because of its over-emphasis on intellection (D428).

Schleiermacher believed that Schelling's error was the opposite of Fichte's error. Schelling's system was also one-sided, but here it was the intellect rather than nature that was not adequately addressed. According to Schleiermacher, Schelling had overlooked the efficacy of the *I* as a moral agent determining the world.[78] Concerning this, Schleiermacher stated in his *Drittes Tagebuch* that Schelling had intended his transcendental philosophy and his natural philosophy to be eternally opposing, but nevertheless equally corresponding, points of view. Accordingly, Schelling's transcendental philosophy ought to clarify the exterior world for the *I*, and his natural philosophy ought to clarify the *I* for the exterior world.

Schelling's speculative physics, which gives the principles of his natural philosophy, ought, thereby, to have as its corresponding equivalent a speculative doctrine of mind [*Geistlehre*], which is an outgrowth and further development of the principles of idealism Schleiermacher believed that no such system was found in Schelling's work.[79]

This negative assessment of the work of both Fichte and Schelling served as an important benchmark in the development of Schleiermacher's own work. The *Dialektik* is, in part, an attempt by Schleiermacher to establish the philosophic foundation for an adequate theory of ethics and physics by using principles that he felt both Fichte and Schelling had inadequately developed.

Dilthey judged Schleiermacher alone among Kant's successors to have held fast to the analytical method of Kant; he offered "not metaphysics, but phenomenology of consciousness."[80] Michael Ermarth, in his book *Wilhelm Dilthey: The Critique of Historical Reason*, cogently summarizes Dilthey's assessment of Schleiermacher. Dilthey thought that Schleiermacher avoided the dualism of Kant, the extremely subjectivist, even solipsistic idealism of Fichte, and the rationalist monism of Hegel by propounding a continuously creative interaction between thought and being, mind and nature, self and world. Contending that Kant and Fichte had given only *formal* autonomy to the subject, Schleiermacher aspired to put the full content of experience in the place of Fichte's "empty" transcendental ego. He rebuked existing forms of idealism for portraying *Geist* as active but essentially "empty."[81] Schleiermacher knew that only a model that held identity and difference to be codeterminate factors in thinking could solve the problem of the gap in Kant's critical philosophy.

When Kant made thought an essentially a priori constructive activity in the second edition of his first *Critique*, he left no room for realism, that is, for an ontologically independent reality as a determining factor in this construction.[82] Vleeschauwer contends that this is the way in which "the Critical philosophy of 1787 [became] a reinforced idealism."[83] Vleeschauwer acknowledges that this charge against Kant of a reinforced idealism in the second edition of his *Critique* goes against the "whole tradition of past Kantian scholarship [which] sees there a more powerful realism."

Wolfgang Carl, writing half a century after Vleeschauwer, reaches a similar conclusion. Kant, Carl argues, assumed rather than proved that the rules that govern the self's unity actually correspond to the content of its objects of thought. Writes Carl,

> The error is that one takes a unity that consists in representations, belonging to a unitary subject, to be a unity exhibited by the representations themselves. Whereas the first unity is based on the unity of the thinking subject, the second unity concerns the representation's interconnectedness, which must be specified by reference not to the subject but to the content of the representations. The first kind of unity can be realized without the second one.[84]

Carl, like Vleeschauwer, also takes the received tradition of Kantian scholarship to task. Carl notes that "[m]odern commentators have referred to Kant's deduction of the categories as 'the mystery' or as 'the jungle'."[85] This is problematic because the "cornerstone" of Kant's reasoning —his notion of apperception—is revealed therein.[86] This cornerstone refers to the self's awareness of itself, unmediated by sensible intuitions, as the same unity of consciousness. This self-awareness is pure thinking. It is thinking aware of itself solely by means of thinking. This "cornerstone" of Kant's reasoning, as such, is the apperceived unity of the self (subject) as the act of thinking—as that which combines the objects of thought. This manner of relating all of the self's representations to itself generates the representation 'I think' in the subject. This designation represents the subject's "perception" of itself as thinking.[87]

Kant refers to this ongoing unity of the selfsame consciousness as "one universal self-consciousness." Writes Kant,

> For the manifold representations, which are given in an intuition, would not be one and all *my* representations, if they did not all belong to one self-consciousness. As *my* representations (even if I am not conscious of them as such) they must conform to the condition under which alone they *can* stand together in one universal self-consciousness, because otherwise they would not all without exception belong to me. (B132–33)

This "one universal self-consciousness" is the foundation of Kant's theory of the objectivity of the pure categories of the understanding. All representations must conform to the conditions entailed in the self's constant unity as the selfsame consciousness. Self-consciousness is an ongoing unity that does not shift with its empirical circumstance. This is the universal that remains constant in all actual knowledge.

As we have seen, Kant's delineation of this one universal self-consciousness was problematic. His discussion entailed a basic ambiguity in his reference to the self. Kant's theory did not acknowledge the difference between the self's actual act of combining disparate elements of thinking (that is, synthesis) and the self's awareness of this unity of thinking, which has been brought about through its own synthesizing activity.

Schleiermacher rejected all delineations of this pure act of the self as sheerly a mental activity. He sought to demonstrate this in his *Dialektik* by delineating the actual nature of the pure act of the self. To do this, he had to establish a standpoint by means of which the pure act of the self could be grasped. Fichte (and J. S. Beck) attempted to establish that same position. While Fichte asked us to "see" it, Schleiermacher expected us to "feel" it.

CHAPTER TWO

Fichte's Insight

Johann Gottlieb Fichte believed that the foundation of Kant's critical philosophy was the self. According to Fichte, the basic fact of consciousness is that throughout our lives, in every moment, we always think "I, I, I" and never anything other than "I."[1] Thus, if there is a determinate thought, there is an 'I' that has determined this thought. This 'I', Fichte argued, is the foundation of Kant's philosophy.

Schleiermacher did not present his first series of lectures on his *Dialektik* until 1811, fourteen years after Fichte had written the two introductions to his *Wissenschaftslehre*. In 1799, however, Schleiermacher did meet Fichte, who had recently moved to Berlin. Schleiermacher had already begun to study Fichte's work and eagerly looked forward to intense philosophic discussions with Fichte. This wish was soon dashed.

Six months after meeting Fichte and dining with him regularly, Schleiermacher in a letter to his friend C. G. von Brinkmann summarized the event. Schleiermacher wrote:

> I had indeed got acquainted with Fichte—who is no longer here at this point, but he did not make much of an impression on me. . . . Before he came, I had the idea of talking about his philosophy and of making known to him my opinion that it does not seem correct to me to separate the ordinary standpoint from philosophy in the way he does. But I soon furled this sail, however. Since I saw how ensconced in the flesh he is in his natural mode of thinking and since I had nothing from which to draw on the matter

within his philosophy, and wondering at something is for
me no object for dialogue and beyond this wondering there
is nothing else than the entirely customary point of contact,
we have not got very close to each other. He is not informa-
tive, for he does not seem to have detailed information
from other sciences—so, too, in philosophy, insofar as
information exists in it—but only general overviews such
as anyone among us has them. This is a great pity, moreover, because he has an absolutely magnificent gift for
making himself clear and he is the greatest dialectician I
know.[2]

Schleiermacher's personal and philosophic disapproval of Fichte in
this letter is obvious. Dilthey notes that the personal style and scientific character of Fichte and Schleiermacher were most decidedly
antithetical and their mutual relationship became increasingly
antipathetic as Schleiermacher developed his own philosophy.
According to Dilthey, "To [their] personal antithesis corresponded a
scientific antithesis, since the world-view of both men was fully
expressive of their character."[3]

   Albert Blackwell, in his book *Schleiermacher's Early Philosophy of
Life*, also discusses Schleiermacher's personal attitude toward
Fichte, noting that after a year's personal acquaintanceship with
Fichte, Schleiermacher stated in a letter to A. W. Schlegel: "We are
on the best of footings with each other—insofar as no footing is still a
footing."[4] Two years later, in 1802, Schleiermacher wrote an equally
caustic letter to Henriette Herz about Fichte's philosophy: "I am
now on to Fichte, and could get a pretty tight hold on him if it were
not such an exhausting maneuver to admire a person and in the
same breath despise him."[5]

   Why then was Fichte of such great concern to Schleiermacher?
Schleiermacher deemed Fichte to be the first philosopher to have
clearly established the self as the foundation of all knowledge (S27).
This, according to Schleiermacher, is something that Kant did not
achieve. Accordingly, Schleiermacher never took issue with Fichte's
attempt to separate out philosophy from the "ordinary standpoint."
He simply deemed Fichte's attempt to do so a failure.

   Schleiermacher's praise of Fichte's insight was thus double-
edged: He gave him credit as the first philosopher to have *clearly*
established the self as the source of all theories of ethics in particular
and philosophy in general; but he simultaneously dismissed Fichte's

own philosophic system, claiming that when all was said and done, Fichte had in fact accomplished nothing (S27).

Schleiermacher's conclusion is not surprising, because as Dieter Henrich has suggested in his essay "Fichte's Original Insight," Fichte did not discover a fact but a difficulty.[6] Accordingly, Fichte's insight rather than his own philosophic system is his most important legacy to Western philosophy. Fichte realized that "'self-consciousness,' which philosophy long before him had claimed to be the basis of knowledge, can be conceived only under conditions that had not been considered previously."[7] Kant had not considered these conditions. Therefore, Kant's theory of the self, rather than the self per se, was the problem.[8]

In this present chapter, our examination of Fichte's insight will function as a bridge from the Kantian problematic both he and Schleiermacher sought to solve to Schleiermacher's own resolution of this problem. I will focus on the special "frame of mind" or "standpoint" both Fichte and J. S. Beck believed were necessary to resolve the apparent gap in Kant's theory of the self. According to Fichte, he and Beck were the only Kantians[9] who understood Kant's highest principle.[10] Only they understood that to "see" Kant's "highest principle in the whole sphere of human knowledge" required a requisite standpoint, without which Kant's philosophy is finally unintelligible. Our present task is to examine this "requisite standpoint."

Our purpose in undertaking this examination is twofold. First, this investigation will serve as an introduction to a nonconceptual and noncognizable "highest standpoint," which Schleiermacher believed was necessary in order to "traverse the gap" in Kant's theory and retrieve the self that links thinking to the organic world. As we shall see, Schleiermacher found the standpoint Fichte delineated, as well as the language he developed to explain it, inadequate. Schleiermacher constructed his own requisite standpoint and language in the wake of what he deemed to be Fichte's own failed work. The basic premise of this chapter is that if we are to understand Schleiermacher's endpoint, we must understand where he began.

In this chapter, I will not discuss the respective philosophies that Beck and Fichte subsequently developed from their elucidations of Kant's critical philosophy. Their *standpoints* and not their actual *philosophies* serve as a useful propaedeutic for Schleiermacher's own standpoint. It is interesting to note, however, that

Beck called Fichte's subsequent system "nonsense."[11] Fichte, on the other hand, did not dismiss Beck's philosophic work but simply relegated it to being a stepping stone to his own system. Fichte believed that Beck's work had value as a propaedeutic that would clear the way for Fichte's more original insight.[12]

Second, our investigation will demonstrate why attempts to establish such a requisite standpoint have been notoriously difficult for Western philosophers to comprehend. For his own effort, Fichte, not surprisingly, has been called "one of the greatest obscure philosophers we have had."[13] John H. Taber, for instance, in his book *Transformative Philosophy: A Study of Sankara, Fichte and Heidegger*, argues that Fichte's obscurity is due to his attempt not simply to reorder our familiar experience but to expand it by introducing another dimension to experience in which the fundamental relationship between knower and known has been altered such that the effect brings about a total transformation in consciousness.[14] In a much more restrained and circumspect manner, Dieter Henrich hints at the same obscurity and nonintelligibility that is inherent in Fichte's standpoint, suggesting that "Philosophers have forgotten [Fichte's original insight]; worse still, they have never taken notice of it."[15]

Fichte believed that he actually saw the missing link between the noumenal and phenomenal self in Kant's critical philosophy and endeavored to teach others how to see it by means of a requisite standpoint, which he called "intellectual intuition." To understand the requirements for such a standpoint, we are going to have to understand four basic claims made by Fichte. We must understand why Fichte believed that

- Kant's critical philosophy had a foundation. As Fichte suggested in the second introduction to his *Wissenschaftslehre*: "For me, in no way is the *Critique of Pure Reason* lacking in foundations. It very clearly placed them there. But they have not been assembled [*aufgebaut*] and the building-materials—although already neatly prepared—are placed next to and superimposed on one another in the manner of a very arbitrary order."[16]
- The foundation of Kant's system was the self. According to Fichte, Kant had deduced the a priori categories of understanding from this ever-present *I*.
- Kant actually had established a system for tying together all of human knowledge although Kant never actually specified it.[17]

- Without a requisite standpoint, the highest principle of Kant's philosophy is unintelligible.

Fichte, like the Austrian philosopher Karl Leonard Reinhold, had attempted to make the first principle of philosophy something living—the actuality of consciousness. Although Reinhold and Fichte never met, they did correspond. Fichte freely acknowledged his debt to Reinhold's pioneering work. In his first letter to Reinhold, Fichte acknowledged how very much he "discerned and revered" Reinhold's "pure love of truth" and "his ardent [warmes] interest in everything which is of highest importance to humanity."[18]

Fichte and Reinhold also acknowledged their differences. Fichte, for instance, in his second letter to Reinhold, stated that their philosophic approaches were not always in agreement and that they were on different paths. Nevertheless, they were united in their quest, that is, their effort to achieve the same goal.[19] Reinhold also noted their differences in his response to Fichte's work, *Über den Begriff der Wissenschaftslehre*.[20] Reinhold confessed that he had not understood most of it and feared "that the man himself, except for his field of vision, had lost value for [Reinhold]."[21]

Fichte's "field of vision" is that which the two philosophers shared. This field of vision pertained to human consciousness as the foundation and first principle for philosophic inquiry. The first principle of philosophy, they both claimed, was not merely a concept, a presupposition of thinking; rather, it was something living—that which engenders all concepts. Fichte, for instance, in his *Wissenschaftslehre* of 1794, affirmed that even the most certain of philosophic principles, that is, the principle of identity (A = A), is based on the identity of the self. This principle of identity, Fichte argued, is merely the abstraction of the actual content (i.e., the self) from the mere form in which this content is given.[22]

Schleiermacher studied Fichte in order to ascertain the adequacy of the standpoint proposed by Fichte to experience this living content of the self. Schleiermacher rejected Fichte's standpoint and established his own, believing that Fichte had simply rendered evident and explicit the implicit logic in Kant's theory of the ongoing unity of the self as a thinking thing.

Fichte's problem, from Schleiermacher's perspective, was simple: Fichte had not escaped the perpetual circle of Kant's logically simple subject. Kant's 'I' signified a logically simple subject that the very concept of thought entails. (B404; B407; A346) Accordingly, any judgment that attempts to determine the content of this 'I' simply begs the question. This is the "perpetual circle" in which Kant's logical subject was caught. From this standpoint, any attempt to get beyond it became a paralogism, a "proof" that assumed what it sought to prove. This is the paralogism Schleiermacher believed Fichte failed to overcome.

Schleiermacher discussed his difficulties with Fichte's philosophic determination of the 'I' in a review of Fichte's *Bestimmung des Menschens* [*The Determination of Humanity*].[23] Fichte's problem, Schleiermacher suggested, is indicated by the very title of the book.

> How can someone who believes in the freedom and the continuity of the self [*Selbstständigkeit*], or who even only wishes to so believe, how can such a person ask about a "determination of humanity?" What can this question mean if one has first asked "What am I?"[24]

Schleiermacher's point is that the generality "humanity" is not an adequate answer to a question of self-inquiry. Rather, the answer to such inquiry must be a particular determination of the 'I': an individual, a *Dasein*, something existent, a specific state of being of the questioner. Fichte argues, Schleiermacher suggests, that all *Dasein* is only for the sake of reason. Accordingly, becoming and doing [*Machen*] are also only for and by means of reason.[25] But how, Schleiermacher asks, can one separate the question "What am I?" from reason?

According to Schleiermacher, Fichte does so by referring to the 'I''s original awareness of itself by means of thought of the moral law. This being the case, the 'I' is originally aware of itself not as *Dasein* but as thought, specifically, thought of the moral law. Fichte's answer, Schleiermacher continues, can only be further delineated by asking the Kantian question "What is the highest good?"[26] Any other approach to a determination of humanity leads either to a discussion of nature, which Fichte does not wish, or to a method of determination of humanity, which Schleiermacher finds untenable. Thus, Schleiermacher's misgivings [*Zweifel*] about Fichte's philosophic method greatly tempered his praise of Fichte's original insight.

It is important to note here that Wilhelm Dilthey, in the first volume of his *Leben Schleiermachers*,[27] notes the Fichtean influence on Schleiermacher's *Dialektik*. Dilthey first notes that Fichte sought a common ground for Kant's theoretical and practical philosohies and found it in the absolute identity of the subject and object in the 'I''s act-of-thinking. Dilthey then argues that Schleiermacher accepted this Fichtean process. Writes Dilthey,

> The Dialektik of Schleiermacher accepts this step. It searches for a transcendental ground for our certainty in knowledge, i.e., for the conviction that a being corresponds to thought and for our certainty in the act-of-desiring to know [*Wollen*] i.e., that the being is responsive to and homogeneous with the thought and finds it in the identity of the ideal and the real.[28]

Fichte's positive legacy to Schleiermacher, Dilthey here argues, is Schleiermacher's search in his *Dialektik* for whatever surety we may have in our knowledge. This transcendental ground for both Fichte and Schleiermacher pertains to an undemonstrable *conviction* that lies beyond the grasp of concepts.[29]

In his second volume, Dilthey further notes something else that both Fichte and Schleiermacher have in common: Kant. According to Dilthey, Schleiermacher's *Dialektik* rests upon the fundamental Kantian idea that there is no metaphysics exceeding the world of empirical experience. Rather, "where any actual thinking is, it is there linked with the matter [*Materie*] of our experience."[30] Dilthey then notes that the work of Fichte rests upon this same fundamental Kantian idea. He concludes that the philosophies of both Fichte and Schleiermacher, as theories of knowledge, are "only a development out of the insights of Kant's *Critique of Reason*."[31] The position that I am developing in this book is in basic agreement with these general claims by Dilthey.

Our analysis begins with Beck, a mathematician who was Kant's friend and most brilliant student. During the early 1790s, Kant and Beck corresponded, and Kant's comments about Beck's developing insights were highly favorable. Fichte valued Beck's work as a propaedeutic that would clear the way for Fichte's own more original insight.[32] We will use Beck as an introduction to Fichte, whom Schleiermacher believed, as we have seen, was the greatest dialectician he had ever met. Our goal is to make intelligible the claim by both Beck and Fichte that a nonconceptualizable frame of mind is necessary if one is adequately to understand Kant's theory of the self. Only then will we be able to understand Schleiermacher's own attempt to delineate a more adequate but equally noncognizable standpoint. This noncognizable state of the self, as we shall see, is both the problem and the solution that Beck, Fichte, and Schleiermacher sought to affirm.

Beck's Standpoint: Original Reconciliation

During the course of their correspondence in the early 1790s, Kant urged Beck to write a summary of the critical philosophy for the general public. By 1794, Beck had written two volumes summarizing Kant's work. Based on a new insight, Beck now considered writing a third volume. In his letter to Kant dated June 17, 1794, Beck laid out an initial summary of his new insight and mentioned the possibility of writing a third volume of Kant's work based on this new insight. Beck sought Kant's opinion as to the advisability of such a project.[33]

Kant's reply was cautiously qualified but basically positive. Kant confessed that in writing his response to Beck's letter, he was aware of his own lack of clarity on the matters at hand. Kant asked for further clarification of Beck's term "original reconciliation [*Ursprüngliche Beylegung*]" and reminded Beck that synthesizing is not something given to us but something done by us. Kant concluded by wishing Beck luck in achieving a simple presentation of these topics in his new book and urged his "dear friend" to "stay within the boundaries of clarity."[34]

Beck, in his letter, had suggested that the synthetic unity of apperception, identified by Kant as the highest point of transcendental philosophy and as that to which all of logic and all employment of the understanding must be ascribed (B134), entailed a twofold activity of understanding. Kant, in the second edition of his first *Critique*, had identified his supreme principle—the synthetic unity of apperception—as an act of understanding. This act entails two processes: (1) all representations that are given to the self must stand under this synthesis, and (2) all representations that are given to the self must first have been created by this synthesis (B135). Kant called this twofold process the "supreme principle of all employment of the understanding" (B136) and "the highest principle in the whole sphere of human knowledge" (B135).

Kant also claimed that we can be conscious of this twofold process. Kant supported this contention by analyzing the claim that I am conscious of myself as always the same 'I' with respect to the manifold of representations that are given to me in an intuition (B135). What, Kant is implicitly asking, is presupposed by this fact that "I call them one and all *my* representations" (B135)? His answer is that such a claim means that

> I am conscious to myself *a priori* of a necessary synthesis of representations—to be entitled the original synthetic unity of apperception—under which all representations that are given to me must stand, but under which they have also first to be brought by means of a synthesis. (B135–136)

Beck called this twofold process "Original Reconciliation." According to Beck, this activity first creates the means by which consciousness can be achieved. It first creates the concept of an object for the understanding. Without the concept, consciousness of an object is impossible. Next, this activity produces the awareness of the conceptualized object. This awareness is expressed in consciousness as the 'I think an object'. The same activity, Beck suggested, thus generates concepts and produces consciousness by means of the reconciliation through the concepts of that which is conceptualized.

Beck believed that this twofold activity of understanding could not be grasped through concepts because this activity is preconceptual. It is prior to concepts, creates concepts, and produces concepts. Accordingly, to become aware of this activity a person cannot use concepts. Rather, the person must enter into a certain frame of mind, a certain mode of thinking that is preconceptual but nevertheless is an actual state of the mind. In other words, the person must acquire a requisite standpoint that allows one to *notice* this twofold, preconceptual activity of understanding—the creation and production of concepts—as it happens.

Simply stated, for Beck, the apparent equivocation in Kant's critical philosophy was based on a twofold operation entailed in any act of understanding. Kant's system seemed to "wobble" only because this one act entailed both a process and a product of this process. If the twofold nature of this act could actually be "seen" as it took place, the justification for the "instability" in Kant's use of terms to describe this one activity would have been found and the ambiguous nature of Kant's description of the self's own agency would be explained. According to Beck, this requisite standpoint for seeing this process would render the "supreme principle" of Kant's critical philosophy more accessible.

Kant, as was noted above, had originally asked Beck to make the critical philosophy more accessible to the general public. Beck now saw his new insight simply as a continuation of this same project originally undertaken at the master's behest. Beck also believed that a clear delineation of the requisite standpoint could provide readers of Kant's philosophy with the key that would unlock the meaning of Kant's entire transcendental philosophy. Beck explained this activity in detail in his *Standpunct*,[35] the subsequently published third volume of his ongoing explication of Kant's critical philosophy.

In this volume, Beck reminds us that we have a concept of a *bond* between the objects of our thoughts and that to which these objects refer.[36] To what objective fact does our *concept* of the bond refer? According to Beck, our concept refers to the synthetic objective unity of consciousness.[37] Beck argues that without understanding this referent, we can never adequately understand the connection between the representation in consciousness of an object and what this representation represents.[38]

Beck suggests that in order to see that to which the concept of the connection between the representation and its Object refers, one must have reached the standpoint of a transcendental philosophy.[39] This standpoint was revealed in the highest principle of Kant's first *Critique*—his synthetic unity of apperception.[40] Those who understand this principle understand that the bond between a representation and its Object is not another representation. Rather, the bond is the synthetic unity of consciousness.[41]

According to Beck, we must "enter into" the frame of mind in which we can "see" how concepts are born. We must see that the categories are nothing other than original modes of representation [*Vorstellungsarten*].[42] This is Beck's "postulate," which each of us must "take on." A *proposition*, Beck tells us, is the representation of things through concepts.[43] A postulate, on the other hand, does not refer to things. How then do we delineate this particular postulate? According to Beck, such delineation is impossible. Beck acknowledges that he only wishes to delineate the procedure by means of which the spirit of a postulate can be seen. What is a postulate? Writes Beck:

> I do not have an answer. The correct answer is the original act-of-representing itself. I can do nothing more than to indicate to the reader the procedure with which he himself in regard to this must be concerned in order to grasp [*vernehmen*] the spirit of the postulate.[44]

In the *Standpunct*, Beck argues that Kant's first *Critique* teaches us that the categories make experience possible. These categories, however, are simply the original modes of representation [*das ursprüngliche Vorstellungsarten*]. These original modes are constituted by the spontaneous act of understanding. Beck characterizes this act as an act of representing [*Vorstellen*]. Such acts constitute the modes of representation that are Kant's categories. According to Beck, the necessary and universal bond between the pure categories and their application to Objects lies in the fact that the pure concepts presuppose an original act of representing [*Vorstellen*].[45]

According to Beck, a principle is "a cognition which grounds other cognitions."[46] As such, the absolutely highest principle in philosophy must be the ground for all other philosophic principles and uses of reason. This highest principle, according to Beck, "says absolutely nothing and yet nevertheless is the ground of all possible statements."[47] This is so, Beck argues, because the highest principle of philosophy can have absolutely no other form than that of a postulate—a call to a certain stance or position (a standpoint) by means of which, when achieved, the ground of all possible expressions of reason is known.[48] How does the application of the categories to Objects occur? The answer to this question cannot be delineated by means of concepts because the answer itself pertains to that which precedes conception. Nevertheless, we do have access to the answer. We can open our "mind's eye" to that which makes the objective validity of our concepts possible. We cannot conceive of it, nor grasp it by means of sensible intuition. We must move beyond Kant's words in order to perceive the truth of his principle.[49]

All concepts are derived, Beck is arguing, and as such cannot be the basis for absolute certainty. The justification for universal certainty can rest only on actual facts. Such "facts," Beck concludes, refer not to that to which the concept refers but that which is beyond and prior to the concept, that is, the original act of representing.[50] This, according to Beck, is what Kant means when he writes about the synthetic unity of apperception. To understand Kant's meaning, we must first experience the actual occurrence to which the bond refers. We can do this only by looking within ourselves beyond our concepts to the original synthetic activity of understanding itself. This experience is the only justification for universal certainty.

Beck established the missing link in Kant's system as a bond that can be "seen" but not conceptualized. His call to a certain standpoint is simply the invitation to see this link that cannot be otherwise known. This experience, however, entails neither concepts nor sensations. It is this call to see this link that marks the place which Beck, Fichte, and Schleiermacher each sought to elucidate in their own independently formulated philosophies.

Fichte's Standpoint: Intellectual Intuition

As with Beck, Kant also initially granted favored status to Fichte. Kant played a special role in Fichte's first major work, *Attempt at a Critique of All Revelation*; Kant recommended it for publication. Published anonymously by Kant's own publisher, the manuscript was mistakenly assumed to be a new work by Kant. This mistake, when discovered, raised the young Fichte to the rank of a major new Kantian philosopher.

According to Fichte, true philosophical idealism entails two points of view: (1) the philosopher's observations and disclosures of the structures of the activity of the I, and (2) the self-revealing structuring activity of the I itself. The critics of idealism fail to make a distinction between these two points of view.[51] Failing to make this distinction, the idealist's mode of thinking is construed as being a demand to accept *in life* this philosophic perspective *on life*.[52] But this is an absurd demand, Fichte claims, because *life* is the activity of the self's activity, that is, the activity of the cogitating I.

Fichte argues here that even among those who profess philosophical idealism, some fail to understand the two points of view entailed in idealism. Failing to take this dual perspective into account, they call for an accompanying realist system exterior to the idealist system. But this is absurd, because no such realist system can be founded distinct from human experience (although various positivists and other empiricists have presumed to do so). The I must always be included in any such discussion if the discussion is to be anything more than empty notions. In other words, there is no such thing as a thing-in-itself separable from the self-positing-I.[53]

Life is the I's experiences. Life, in this way, stands in contradistinction to the philosophic view that contemplates it. In other words, the pure activity of the I is life itself. Concepts of this activity—an objectification of this activity—is a restriction or determination of an aspect of life.

The I, according to Fichte, stands over against all that it thinks. All that it thinks = the manifold of presentation. Accordingly, the I stands over against the manifold of presentation. The I presupposes it.[54] Two perspectives are entailed here: the I and that which the I stands over against—the manifold of its presentations. The dogmatist knows only the latter perspective. For the dogmatist, there are only things—an objective world. There is an I to the extent that it apprehends this objective world. Such a position entails one perspective: that of things impacting upon the I. This perspective is that of the thing which is being thought about.

A major source of misunderstanding and many ill-fitting [*nichts passenden*] objections to his work can be laid at the feet of either the failure to distinguish the two distinct processes employed in idealist and dogmatic philosophy, or the confusion of that which belongs in one system with that which belongs in the other. Such errors can only be made by dogmatic philosophers, Fichte concludes. It is they who encounter only one intellectual process in their observations.[55] Having no experience with a double intellectual process, they interpret this double process as if it really entails only one intellectual action.

The cost of this dogmatic failure of perception has been great. Not only, Fichte claims, has his *Wissenschaftslehre* been distorted and misrepresented by others for this very reason, but so, too, has the work of the great master himself: Kant. The widespread acceptance of the dogmatists' distortions of Kant's first *Critique*, Fichte asserts:

> will remain forever in the annals of philosophy as the ignominy [*Schande*] of our century, and our descendants will be able to clarify the events of this period [*Jahr*] not otherwise than through the presupposition of a mental epidemic [*Geistesepidemie*] which propagated itself in this period.[56]

The philosopher's first task is self-contemplation. He[57] must think about his act of thinking. In this way, he observes his I disclosing itself. This disclosure is the pure activity of the I. This activity is life itself, existence in itself.[58] Accordingly, life stands in contradistinction to the philosopher's contemplation of it. Life is distinct from the observations of it. In other words, the philosopher notices, in self-contemplation, that his I always remains the same.

The first question for the idealist philosopher is thereby: How is the I for itself the selfsame?[59] Simply put, the first question is: How is it that I am always the selfsame I? How is it that $I = I$, that *I am I* regardless of the specific determinate activity of the I?

The fact that the I does in fact remain the same (that is, *I am I*) is, according to Fichte, the absolutely basic, first principle of all knowledge. Fichte maintains that this is Kant's most basic principle, even though Kant never specifically stated it. This principle, Fichte argues, is the means by which Kant deduced the categories.[60]

Fichte acknowledges that Kant never proved that he had derived his categories from this principle. Kant never systematically demonstrated the way in which the categories were derived.[61] Kant's critical philosophy, accordingly, is not complete. Fichte believed that Kant knew this. Fichte cites the following sentence from Kant's *Critique* as an example: "In this treatise, I purposely omit the definitions of the categories, *although I may be in possession of them* (B108—Kemp Smith translation)."[62] Simply stated, Fichte here argues that Kant's *Critique of Pure Reason* is not a *system* of pure reason. But, Fichte continues, Kant never claimed to have presented such a completed system.[63] Nevertheless, one can find in Kant's *Critique*, Fichte continues, the foundations upon which such a system can be built.

Like Beck, Fichte believed that all concepts are derived. Accordingly, certainty based on concepts is never absolute, but is always a conditioned, mediated certainty. Demonstration by means of concepts cannot produce absolute certainty.[64] Fichte's *Wissenschaftslehre* pertains to that which the concept presupposes, that is, the original act of representing. In this original act, the self is neither subject nor object. As the subject, we are aware of that which we reflect as a limitation [*Beschränktheit*] upon our intelligence. This "narrow-mindedness" is caused by the object. Because of it, we can only think the finite. Accordingly, we know ourselves only as finite. Or, if we are aware of ourselves only as the object, we know ourselves as limited, restricted. We know ourselves only as finite and accordingly can only think the finite.[65]

But such a division of the self into subject and object, Fichte argues, clarifies nothing. This is so because the I of the original act-of-representing is neither subject nor object alone, but the union of both. Concerning this, Fichte states: "Originally, I am neither the reflecting nor the reflected and neither one is determined through the other. On the contrary, I am *both in their union*, which union I, of course, cannot think, because precisely in thinking do I separate the reflected and the reflecting."[66]

This original act is an "undivided moment" of the I.[67] Our awareness of ourselves as neither subject nor object but the union of both is *intellectual intuition*. According to Fichte, intellectual intuition is the foundation of the concept. We do not originate anything when we think. Rather, we can only think that which has been immediately intuited. Thinking that is not based on intuition and that does not include an abiding intuition in the same identical moment is an empty activity. Actually, it is not thinking at all.[68]

All self-consciousness presupposes this original activity of the I, that is, the sheer activity of the I returning back to itself.[69] This primordial act of the I returning to itself makes consciousness possible but is itself not a part of consciousness. It is a pure activity that in its self-reflectiveness posits both itself and that which is different from itself. This same act, according to Fichte, posits both identity and difference.

Thinking, Fichte argues, entails antithesis, a reflecting and a reflected, a subject and object. Intellectual intuition is conceptualized by means of its opposite, by mediated awareness. Writes Fichte, "I determine my intuition through thinking an antithesis to myself. The expression 'I comprehend the intuition' means this and nothing other than this."[70] In other words, thinking is the comprehension of the self by means of that which is antithetical to it. The self, as we have seen, is both the subject and object. Thinking about the self divides it into subject and object. Thinking, thus, can grasp the self only by means of the juxtaposition of its antithetical parts. By so doing, the original unity which the division presupposes is sundered. The original unity of the self is comprehended in intellectual intuition. The presupposition of this original unity is that upon which all concepts rest.

Not surprisingly, the first principle of Fichte's *Wissenschaftslehre* is a postulate rather than a concept. It is a call, an invitation. Fichte's postulate invites the philosopher to self-contemplation. The postulate is: "think of yourself, construct the concept of this self just thought of and notice how you do this."[71]

Three steps are entailed in this postulate. Step one is the actual turn of thinking to itself as its own object. Step two is the process of conceptualizing this turning of thinking to itself. Step three is the call to study the process by means of which step two occurs.

The first step invites the philosopher to observe the pure I; this is the self as the act of thinking. The first step is the call to observe this act. According to Fichte, the pure I is different from the philosopher's own determinate experiences.[72] These latter experiences

pertain to his *conscious relationship* to the act of thinking rather than
to thinking per se.

The philosopher, in step one, is being invited to observe the
actual act of thinking. By so doing, he observes thinking returning to
thinking. In this process, he realizes that thinking is nothing other
than this self-referring activity. He has discovered that nothing more
belongs to thinking than "the returning back into itself of thinking
[*das Zurückkehren in sich*]."[73]

According to Fichte, this self-returning act is a sheer act prior to
all consciousness. The philosopher's awareness of it, thereby, is a
sheer immediate awareness—an intuition [*Anschauung*].[74] Fichte has
called our *immediate awareness* of this precondition to consciousness
intellectual intuition. "That there is such a faculty of intellectual intuition," Fichte argued,

> cannot be demonstrated, nor can what it is be developed
> from concepts. Each person must find it immediately in
> himself, or he will never learn to know it. The demand that
> one ought to demonstrate it through reasoning, is much
> more astounding than would be the demand that one must
> explain what colors are to someone who has been born
> blind.[75]

Fichte believed that Kant's notion of *pure apperception* was in
fact this standpoint, which Fichte sought to delineate in his
Wissenschaftslehre. According to Fichte, "The intellectual intuition of
which the *Wissenschaftslehre* speaks, absolutely does not at all arise
out of a being, but out of an action [*Handeln*], and it is not at all
referred to by Kant (except, if one will, through the expression *pure
apperception*)."[76] Beck, as was noted above, also made Kant's
"supreme principle" the reference for the "highest standpoint" of
philosophy.

With the second step of Fichte's postulate, the philosopher not
only intuits [*anschaut*] but also comprehends [*begreift*].[77] Here, the
philosopher has formed a concept of the activity that has just
occurred. He has conceptualized a moment of the pure I, of the act of
self-returning. This concept is not the I's pure activity. As such, the
concept is '*not-I.*' In other words, it is a *concept* of the pure I rather
than the pure I itself. The concept is not the self. Accordingly, the
concept = not-self.

With step three, the philosopher now realizes that all distinc-
tions that are posited by himself as distinct from himself are in fact
self-determinations of himself. In other words, the concept is a

determination of the self. The philosopher has discovered that he is at one and the same time both subject and object.[78]

❖ ❖ ❖

What does Fichte mean by "posits"? His response to this question is reminiscent of Beck's response when asked to elucidate the first postulate of his *Standpunct*. According to Fichte, his words are simply a formula. Writes Fichte:

> The I posits itself purely and simply; it is at once a subject and an object. But this is not an adequate description of the I. It is no more than a formula, and for those who do not breathe life into it by an inner intuition which they themselves produce, it remains an empty, dead, and unintelligible figure of speech. An inner act is required of the student of the *Wissenschaftslehre*. He is requested "to be subject and object at once," so that he can discover the identity in question within himself. . . . With its first proposition the *Wissenschaftslehre* succeeds in establishing not just philosophy in its entirety but also the conditions for all philosophizing.
>
> This science simply cannot do anything to convince anyone who does not wish to satisfy this condition, that is, who will not produce an intuition of his own I within himself. . . . [I]t cannot provide him with a truth which cannot be provided from without and which one has to produce within oneself. This is something that not even God himself can do.[79]

This is Fichte's original insight: The original act of the self is reflexive but not a reflection. The original act is the self returning to itself. This original act precedes consciousness and is the unity of the self as both subject and object. As Henrich demonstrates in his essay "Fichte's Original Insight," this insight of Fichte's replaced Kant's theory of the self as reflection with a theory of the self as positing.

Fichte realized that the circularity that Kant claimed as inherent in all explorations of the original *I-act* indicated the inadequacy of Kant's theory rather than the impossibility of actually exploring the original activity itself.[80] Fichte, Henrich argues, was the first philosopher to recognize Kant's perpetual circle as a problem pertaining to *Kant's* theory of the self and then to draw consequences from it in erecting a new theory of the self.[81]

The formal distinction between Kant's and Fichte's theories of the self, as Henrich demonstrates, is that in Kant's theory, the two I's [thinking and consciousness] already presuppose their relationship and as "relata" are given equal value. Fichte, on the other hand, intends his theory to explain rather than simply to presuppose a relationship and he distinguishes the original act from that which it produces. Only the original act is recognized as the highest principle of philosophy. Only its product (consciousness) can be classified as knowledge. The reflexive act is, for Fichte, the actual act of positing. Consciousness, reflection, is its product. Nevertheless, both "relata," as Fichte attempts to delineate in the ongoing development of his theory, become actual, simultaneously.[82]

Fichte's *Wissenschaftslehre* is his systematic deduction of the implications discovered in an immediate moment of intellectual intuition. From this moment, our understanding of identity and difference is born.[83] Fichte intends his transcendental philosophy to demonstrate that everything in consciousness arises through self-consciousness and refers back to the primordial self-referring act of the I.[84]

How, Henrich asks repeatedly, as he traces Fichte's development of his original insight through the various stages of his *Wissenschaftslehre*, does this knowledge become intelligible? Henrich convincingly demonstrates that Fichte's repeated efforts to answer the question failed. Henrich argues that in the end Fichte, like Kant, did not succeed in demonstrating the structure of self-consciousness that makes it possible for the I to know itself as an empirical object and thus to achieve consciousness of the world in general.

Fichte, like Kant, had to presuppose knowledge of the I in order for the I to know itself. This presupposition left the gap between thinking and its object unresolved. This was the very complaint that Fichte lodged against Kant's doctrine of the self as a theory of reflection. Fichte's theory found itself caught up in the same perpetual circle that Kant claimed would be faced by anyone who sought to peer into pure apperception and delineate its content.

Schleiermacher's Scant Praise

Schleiermacher accused Fichte of not making enough of the I.[85] According to Schleiermacher, Fichte's method, at best, determined a pure act of doing [*Thuns*], but no Being (S29); it lacked explanatory power for nature, the world, the physical aspect of human experience because Fichte had overlooked human nature, *Dasein*, in the quest for a "higher philosophy."

Fichte, however, believed that he could not and must not go further. According to Fichte,

> My philosophy is here totally independent of all accident, and a product of iron necessity, in as far as necessity takes place for free, unhampered [*frei*] reason, i.e., [as] the product of iron necessity. From this standpoint, I can go no further, because I must not go further. And so transcendental idealism exhibits itself at the same time as the sole mode of thinking in philosophy in conformity with one's duty. Here, speculation and the moral law most intimately unite. I ought to go out from the pure I in my act of thinking [*Denken*], and I ought to consider [*denken*] it absolutely self-active, not as determined through things but as determining things.[86]

To such a method, Schleiermacher responded, "Is not one necessarily obliged to arrive at idealism, as soon as one wishes only to *think* about moralism?"[87] Schleiermacher's answer, of course, was "yes." Fichte's theoretical philosophy thereby mirrored the reflections of the old way. Fichte, Schleiermacher concluded, was an idealist of the old school, who unlike the "new thinkers," among whom Schleiermacher counted himself, disparage being as a state codeterminate with reason. Concerning this, Schleiermacher wrote: "If, for us non-philosophers or natural philosophers, Fichte situates [*stellt*] his theoretical philosophy only upon this point of view, isn't he obliged, from our point of view, to do his philosophy incorrectly?"[88] Fichte's "one-sided method," according to Schleiermacher, prevented him from answering such questions as: How are the I and the not-I one? By what means do they meet? What is the means of their unity? Fichte could not answer these questions, Schleiermacher argued, because Fichte had not determined the means by which the temporal and the eternal, the universal and the particular, the form and the essence, the "that" and the "how" are in one another and are one.[89] He had not determined how speculation and empirical investigation are united and form knowledge. Fichte has no insight into any of this, Schleiermacher argued. Of all such matters, Schleiermacher declared, "Fichte knows nothing."[90] Nor, Schleiermacher continued, will Fichte ever arrive at answers to these questions by means of his method. Anyone who awaits answers from Fichte to such questions must wait in vain.[91] This is the case because Fichte's terms represent rigid [*strenge*] antitheses; he does not know how his I and not-I meet.[92] Schleiermacher concluded that Fichte had arrived at his explanations of the world only by deriving something from nothing.[93]

Schleiermacher thus rejected Fichte's standpoint as inadequate for the self that was "left over" and left out of all philosophic propositions.

Kant's Conflicted Condemnation

Kant, on the other hand, adamantly rejected the call for a higher standpoint by both Fichte and Beck. Kant's outraged response to their exclusivist claim was "May God protect us from our friends." In his "Open letter on Fichte's *Wissenschaftslehre*, August 7, 1799," Kant rejected both Beck's and Fichte's claim that there was a fundamental presupposition, a requisite standpoint that must be grasped if his *Critique* were to be understood. The only standpoint required, Kant insisted, is intelligence, "the common standpoint that any cultivated mind will bring to such abstract investigations."[94]

Kant's rejection of Beck and Fichte's work entailed two elements. The first and most obvious element in Kant's public denouncement of Beck and Fichte was their advocacy of a standpoint needed in order to render his system coherent. Kant's criticism of this standpoint was straightforward. He never wavered in his opposition to the postulation of a requisite standpoint inherent in his transcendental philosophy; he never called upon the reader to enter into a requisite standpoint in order to understand his work. According to Kant, no such transcendental standpoint was necessary. Kant's condemnation of Beck and Fichte in this regard was and remained unambiguous.

Kant's response to a second "offense" incurred by Beck and Fichte was more complex. Beck and Fichte, in their desire for consistency, had discarded Kant's realist postulate that there is indeed a world ontologically distinct from our own constructivist ways of knowing. As we saw in chapter one, Kant, by the end of his life, had wavered in this regard.

Kant's reticence is not surprising because the exegesis of his critical philosophy by Fichte and Beck was, in fact, correct.[95] Kantian scholar Herman-J. de Vleeschauwer masterfully summarizes the rectitude of their claims in his book *The Development of Kantian*

Thought, which I will use as the basis for the following historical reconstruction of the development of Kant's work. I find Vleeschauwer's work useful because it coincides with Schleiermacher's own conclusion regarding the one-sidedness of Kantian and post-Kantian idealism. Vleeschauwer's analysis gives us a historical framework for the development of Kant's thought in this regard.

In 1792, Kant attempted to reorganize his critical philosophy using Beck's principle of *positing together* [*Zusammensetzung*], which has the same meaning as *conjunction* in the *Critique* of 1878.[96] Positing together identifies the only non-sensible factor entailed in the analysis of knowledge; it refers to the way in which the subject constructs the objects of space and time. This principle refers to the pure concept. In his incomplete text *Welches sind die wirklichen Fortschritte die Metaphysik seit Leibnitz's und Wolf's Zeiten in Deutschland gemacht hat?*, sent to a friend in 1800, Kant identifies positing together as the one unique a priori element.

Here Kant, Vleeschauwer suggests, was following Beck's lead. This principle is Kant's principle of identity. But how is diversity now to be explained? How does it arise? How does this function become differentiated? It is evident that it does, because "this originally single function is broken up in its concrete actualization into a number of kinds of acts or of categories." Vleeschauwer suggests that

> The origin of their differentiation cannot be attributed to the unique operation of this *a priori* element which is essentially a source of identity. These differentiations are required to correspond with the sensible presentations of objects in space and in time. That means, it seems to me, that the *a priori* diversity, the foundation of formal intuition, is the principle which differentiates the functions which are distinct from *Zusammensetzung* in general.

Kant, Vleeschauwer argues, never gave "a clear and precise account of the origin of this *a priori* diversity." Based on Kant's own work up to this point, Vleeschauwer concludes that this a priori diversity

> has no other origin than the activity of the logical subject. This means that after all it is Beck and Fichte who are right in their exegesis of the Critical philosophy.[97]

In the first *Critique*, Kant had invited his readers to think about thinking. He called it reflection [*reflexio*] (A260; B316). Kant assured us that by so doing, we could discover the subjective conditions by means of which our thinking produces concepts. We could do this because we would have become conscious of two different kinds of relations. First, we would be conscious of the way in which given representations (that is, the form of thought) are related to our different sources of knowledge. Second, we would be conscious of the actual relation of the different sources of knowledge (that is, the objects of thought) to one another. Kant assured us that we could determine this second relationship by means of the first. As we saw in chapter one, Kant's assurance was premature.

Kant realized that he had not proven that the invariant form of thinking we discover in reflection is necessarily related to the actual objective relationships entailed in our representations. In other words, the unity of the thinking subject had not guaranteed a necessary link of the subject's subjective thoughts to the actual objective relations entailed in the content of empirical knowledge. This disparity between subjective and objective knowledge sundered the self. The thinking self had no guarantee that its knowledge of itself as part of the world of sense actually corresponded to the self's objective reality as part of that empirical, sensate world. The self had no guarantee that it had a body.

The "cornerstone"[98] of this guarantee, as we saw in chapter two, was Kant's notion of apperception. His revised version of the transcendental deduction of the pure categories of the understanding in his first *Critique* rested on the unity of the thinking subject in all of its various acts of constructing the forms by means of which the intuitive world can be known.[99] The element that "totalized" the a priori conditions of the object was the 'I think' or the unity of consciousness.[100] This element was the link between the inner and outer world of the self. In 1798, Kant realized that this element was the weak link in his chain of reasoning.

If Kant had been more "rigorous" in his deduction, a purely logical deduction would have brought the unity of consciousness (form) and the objective structure of the internal relations of the object to the absolute unity of the act of thinking.[101] This absolute unity would have suppressed the distinction between objective and subjective consciousness. Kant was reluctant to do this because of his realist postulate, which affirmed the existence of a world ontologically distinct from the thinking subject. Kant therefore wavered and hesitated in his solution to the gap in his doctrine of the self. "Fichte," Vleeschauwer argues, "did not hesitate."[102]

Fichte's solution was more logical but less human.[103] Fichte suppressed the self that does not pertain to thinking. By so doing, he stripped the subject of its subjective unity of consciousness as a particular, individuated being. This, as we have seen, is the core of Schleiermacher's complaint against Fichte's method. This is also the heart of Vleeschauwer's analysis of the logical rectitude of the work of Beck and Fichte done under the "aegis" of the master's work.

Schleiermacher rejected all such one-sided views of human nature. He knew that all *Dasein* is not only for the sake of reason.[104] Schleiermacher rejected all such philosophies that gave reason such singular privilege. Nevertheless, something about Fichte's standpoint, which *precedes* his actual philosophic work, had caught Schleiermacher's eye. This something was the disclosure of the self that can never be comprehended through concepts, judgments, or sensations. Both Beck and Fichte attempted to establish this noncognizable state of the self as the highest standpoint of philosophy. As we have seen, both philosophers believed that such a standpoint could not be adequately explained. Rather, one must discover it for oneself. Both Beck and Fichte invited the philosopher to do so; only then could the philosopher see far enough to comprehend the "missing link" in Kant's theory of the unity of the self.

Beck and Fichte did not break out of the encased circle of pure thinking. No agency ontologically independent of the logical subject was entailed in their explanation of how the I gives rise to the concepts that link it to its empirical world. Being, as an organic agent distinct from thinking, was left unexplored and unexplained. Kant's realist principle was thereby dashed against the impervious shoals of the rigorous systematic thinking of Beck and Fichte.

Schleiermacher wished to break out of thinking's encased circle and give an account of organic being in its own terms. This was his goal. To do this, he had to establish a standpoint by means of which the physical self (that is, the organic self that is part of the world of nature) could be affirmed in its own terms. But how can he affirm anything that is not thought? All judgments are states of thinking; so, too, are concepts. If he used neither concepts nor judgments, how could he affirm or deny anything, since, according to Schleiermacher, concepts and judgments are our only two forms of thinking? This was the conundrum: Schleiermacher had to devise a way to affirm a state of the self that could not be thought because think-

ing can only affirm itself. Thinking, as such, is a kind of King
Midas—everything it touches turns into a thought. This is the
conundrum that Kant, Beck, and Fichte attempted to overcome:
Kant through his theory about the ether, Beck and Fichte through
their call to "see" with the mind's eye that which cannot be thought.
As we have seen, the attempts by Beck and Fichte pertained sheerly
to an activity of intellection and thus remained encased in thinking,
which cannot reach beyond itself and affirm an organic world.
Kant's attempts "wobbled" because he wished to hold onto his realist principle, which affirms that there are "things" which in their
own terms, are not thinking.

To break out of this encasement and affirm a physical self
(*Dasein*) that is part of the organic world that thinking can never
directly know but can only think about, Schleiermacher had to
devise a vocabulary for consciousness that included a place for the
presence of sheer, noncognizable physicality. In other words, he had
to find a place in consciousness for Kant's realist principle in order to
affirm a reality distinct from human thought. He also had to
describe this noncognizable place in human consciousness in
noncognitive terms. Simply stated, Schleiermacher had to devise a
way of affirming and talking about being without reducing it to
thought. To do this, he devised a master key that opened Kant's circle. Schleiermacher's master key was the elegantly simple realiza-
tion that the circle "In and of itself expresses only mutual
dependence" (D402). With this master key, Schleiermacher established being as something distinct from but codeterminate with
thinking.

CHAPTER THREE

Schleiermacher's New Vocabulary for Consciousness

In the discussion that follows, I shall delineate by means of a recon-struction the way in which Schleiermacher devised and estab-lished the master key that unlocked the perpetual circle that encased the Kantian 'I think'. This discussion is an introduction to Schleier-macher's new vocabulary for self-consciousness developed in his *Dialektik*.

Schleiermacher envisioned his *Dialektik* as his organon for revealing the common features of all thinking and being (D603). His *Dialektik* emerged from his analysis of organic agency as a requisite for determinate thinking. He conceived of this work heuristically as an organon of the process of knowing (D2); thus he had to delineate his analysis of sense perception as an epistemological issue.[1] Accordingly, our discussion begins with a delineation of Schleier-macher's theory of perception. As we shall see, his explanation of the way in which our sense organs are opened and filled is the beginning of his analysis of the twofold nature of an act of thinking.

The Two-fold Nature of an Act of Thinking: The Organic and Intellectual Functions

Schleiermacher first divides thinking into the two ways in which it functions. Thinking functions as (1) that which desires to know and thus opens the sense organs so that they can be filled and as (2) that which determines the sensible data that fill the sense organs so that something can be known. These two operations of thinking together comprise one act of thinking. According to Schleiermacher, "One aspect of the act of the thinking function [*Denkfunction*] without the other gives no complete act of thinking on the way to knowledge" (D432–33).

The concurrence of these two functions constitutes one original act, which consists of the opening and filling of the sense organs (D552n–53n). The content of this act is our organic affections, a mass of impressions shared by the two functions. This mass of sense impressions is thinking-matter. The two functions are the "poles" or "endpoints" between which "knowledge in the process of becoming thinking" takes place (D509). The two functions conjointly determine this mass of impressions by separating it into determinable parts.

Schleiermacher calls the basic power of our mental life to be receptive and thereby organized by that which is exterior to it, our "organic function in thinking." This power is expressed as our actual condition of being stirred in 'organic affections' (D 492). Schleiermacher calls this state of being stirred our condition of being "organically affected" [*Organischafficirtsein*] (D494). This is how he characterizes our ability to sense: according to Schleiermacher, this condition of being organically affected as containing the stuff of thinking, thinking-matter [*Denkstoff*] (D494).

Reason stands in contradistinction to this "matter." Reason is the active agency of our mental life. Schleiermacher calls this ability of our mental life to organize that which is exterior to it, the "intellectual function in thinking." This is the agency that gives form to our chaotic mass of organic affections. It is the "form of thinking" [*Denkform*].

Reason, as the active ground of thinking, is internal to consciousness. Reason has the will to know [*Wissenwollen*] that which is external to it. This will to know is expressed by the activity of reason as the forming of concepts, which is the actual being of thinking. The sheer activity of willing to form concepts, however, is not the actual occurrence of the formation of concepts. Concepts, according to Schleiermacher, are not "innate" to reason (D414). Rather, something must happen to reason in order for the actual construction of a concept to occur. Something other than reason mediates reason's transition from its mere possibility of a concept—the sheer will to form a concept—to its actual construction.

What is it, Schleiermacher wants to know, that shifts the activity of reason from the mere will to conceptualize to the actual construction of a concept? His answer, at its simplest level, is the organic function. Reason, according to Schleiermacher, is only an impulse, a directionless agility (D291n), until it has something upon which to act and concomitantly make distinct by means of separating (D547n). This spontaneous agility is given direction by the strength and weakness of the impulses (D291n) of our organic affections. These organic affections, as we have seen, are the expression of our organic function as the capacity of our mental life to receive that which is external to it. The organic function, as such, interiorly expresses the exterior factor in the act that brings about our organic affections. Schleiermacher calls this act the first affection, which, as we shall see, he defines as the original condition of consciousness.

Consciousness

According to Schleiermacher, the first affection denotes the original condition of consciousness. Schleiermacher defines this affection as

> the (actively thought) opening of the senses as conditioning the influx of effects of the influences of external being [*Außenseins*2].3

This definition gives two determining grounds to consciousness. One is reason; the other is the world.

Our organic affections, in general, are the "stuff" that goes into our mental life. This stuff is our sense impressions and is a result of the impact of the world upon our sense organs. This stuff, however, is not simply external being, nor is it actual thinking; rather, it is an internal expression of a particular capacity of our mental life to be engaged by that which is external to it.

Reason, as the interior ground of consciousness, is the receiving agent for the activity of the organic function. This means that reason's activity is given direction by the active agency of our sense impressions. The organic function, as this efficacious agent of direction-giving, is reason's other. Schleiermacher can now establish a codeterminate relation between reason and sensing, which he does in the following way.

Schleiermacher first establishes a fixed mark or place in consciousness that corresponds to the marked or designated thing that is external to consciousness. He does this by making the determinateness of reason's activity the indicator of the impact on reason by that which is distinct from it. In other words, when reason is given direction, this means that now a determinate place has been established in consciousness for external being, which the particular organic affection (which affected reason) presupposes. This (presupposed) being, indicated by means of the organic affections, is now enclosed [*eingeschloßen*] in the limits of this determinate place in consciousness. The direction given to reason marks this place. This mark in consciousness is the determinate place that Schleiermacher refers to as the "concept" (D235).

Schleiermacher can now define what he means by a concept. A concept is reason's activity of "placing," "locating," or more technically, of "positing" a location in consciousness for a particular group of organic affections. This place, from the standpoint of the organic affection, is the adjustment in activity that reason has made because of the effect on reason by that which is external to it (D498n). The location of our organic affections in consciousness, as we have seen, is the place of intellection. From the standpoint of reason, this location is the beginning of the concept. From the standpoint of the organic function, it is our conscious referent for "things" (D496n–97n). The "thing" brought forth or "determined" is the organic affection that has arisen from the chaotic manifold through the active determination of reason.

Schleiermacher refers to this thing, which has emerged in consciousness, as an "organic concept." This organic concept, from the vantage point of the organic function, is a single individual image— an image that is not itself a concept. In other words, it does not contain other determinable images. The complete determination of this image is the totality of ways in which it can be thought.

Schleiermacher uses the term *consciousness*, in part, to describe the process of concept formation from the perspective of the organic function. Consciousness pertains to the opening and filling of the sense organs. The original condition of consciousness, from the organic perspective, is the undifferentiated manifold of organic affections (D291n).

Consciousness, described from the organic perspective, is *Leiden*, the passive (that is, receptive) capacity of thinking. In its original condition, it is that which is filled with the entangled impressions of the organic affections. From this perspective, the intellectual function is the passive agent; it is that which is being filled. The self-activity of the intellectual function is but a directionless agility in this original condition of consciousness.

The intellectual function is present, but as sheer inner, directionless agility (D547n). In this original state, consciousness is indeterminate consciousness. It is muddled and entangled because the two functions are not in tandem. The will to know [*Wissenwollen*] has not been given determinate direction by the "stimulus [*Reiz*] of consciousness's sense impressions, and the sense impressions have not been selected out and made determinate by the will to know.

Determinate, objective consciousness is always the result of the agency of both functions. Objective consciousness is the result that has been brought to it by the will to know interacting with the manifold of impressions of organic activity.

From the organic function's perspective, (objective) consciousness always pertains to consciousness as Object-dependent. Here, consciousness pertains to the activity of the objects of awareness—to sense images—and, the subject is always the passive agent. The subject is being filled with the activity of the world. Its awareness is the awareness of the way in which the world is impacting upon it. The subject is aware of things. Concerning this, Schleiermacher states in an 1818 lecture, "Out of the original entangledness, we thus see . . . arise . . . consciousness of things [*Dinge*] under the form of images" (D237). This is Schleiermacher's explanation of how perception arises. Our consciousness, from this standpoint, is our awareness of the way in which we are being impacted upon by the sensate world. Our consciousness is aware of sensate "things."

Consciousness of things cannot occur without the perspective of the organic function. From the organic perspective, the "thing" posits. The thing posits itself as a thing. But what has been posited by the intellectual function which is in contradistinction to this thing? This is Schleiermacher's question. Something must have been posited, Schleiermacher argues, otherwise there would not be determination but rather only simple negation. This is so because the intellectual function contains the will to know. It is the activity of reason, the desire to separate [*das Theilenwollen*] so as to discern (D237). It is this activity which, when given determinate direction, brings the system of concepts to consciousness (D235–36). This activity of reason provides the internal direction for the formation of concepts.

Can this activity of reason, Schleiermacher asks, bring forth a real contrast from the sheer indeterminate manifold? From whence does actual, determinate contrast arise (D235)? Certainly not from outside consciousness, for there lies the indeterminate, chaotic manifold. This is the organic function's terrain and no determinate images emerge from the organic affections without the activity of reason. Therefore, the chaotic manifold cannot be the source of the separation [*Theilung*] of this indeterminate world into determinate images.

What, Schleiermacher wants to know, is the source of this separation? What is co-posited by the intellectual function with the organic function's sensible impressions that emerge into consciousness as the individual, determinate images of the world? We cannot look outside consciousness, Schleiermacher argues. The only remaining recourse is to look to self-consciousness for the answer; but what is the actual separation within self-consciousness? It is the separation demonstrated by the *determinate* activity of reason itself—by consciousness (D235–36). In other words, if the activity of reason has been given direction, there is something distinct from this activity that has given reason its direction. If reason has discerned something and is now a determinate activity, there is something that was first given to reason so that it could be discerned. The activity of reason, as we have seen, is conscious only if it is conscious *of* something.

The organic function, therefore, is the other constituting element of consciousness that all conscious (that is, determinate) activity of reason, by the very fact of its determinateness, demonstrates. If there is determinate activity of reason, something has already been given to it to determine.

Schleiermacher argues that this presupposition of organic activity as prior to any determinate activity of reason simply demonstrates the actual distinction between reason and that upon which it acts. This presupposition demonstrates that there is indeed a difference between the activity of reason and the activity of organic affection. Simply stated, the intellectual and the organic functions are not the same. Further, all determinate thinking presupposes that these two functions are codeterminate, if contrasted agencies in this process.

The chaotic totality of sensible impressions (being [*Sein*]) is antithetically placed in contrast to the intellectual function (reason). If this contrast of these two functions were not established as distinct, codeterminate functions, then a person would have to say that reason carries within itself a unity which it then posits as the ground of separation for thinking and being. But this is absurd, Schleiermacher concludes, because it would make the organic function totally superfluous (D234n). Rather, the chaotic manifold of impressions impacts upon the opened senses. This impact upon the senses is the prerequisite for the separation of the original unity of the manifold.

In other words, the organic function delivers [*hergeben*] an indeterminate unity to reason. Reason acts upon this indeterminate unity. The result of reason's activity on this indeterminate unity is a determinate image. This image is the determinate unity, which from the standpoint of the organic function is the first aspect of the building of the concept (D234n). Schleiermacher uses the term *schema* to denote this determinate image, which is the sensible side of the concept. This term denotes both the organic and intellectual functions in the process of concept formation, but from the vantage point of the organic.

Schema designates a particular group of determinable impressions, which has emerged out of the manifold with reason's grasp of the impact of this indeterminate manifold, of impressions upon the senses. "The Schema," according to Schleiermacher, "is only the sensible [*sinnliche*] aspect of the concept" (D209). The image, from the organic standpoint, is a determinate *unity* of impressions, which has emerged from the indeterminate manifold.

This same process, viewed from the standpoint of the intellectual function, issues in a determinate plurality. Like the image, this determinate plurality rests upon a twofold contrast—reason's grasp of the manifold impacting upon the senses. Prior to reason's grasp of the manifold of impressions, reason can only posit an infinite array of possible contrasts, rather than an actual contrast, that is, a determinate plurality. Only with the actual impact of the indeterminate manifold of sensible objects upon the senses does a determinate and therefore actual contrast—a plurality—emerge in reason.

Consciousness arises, Schleiermacher concludes, only out of contrast. Specifically the activity of reason is "placed in contrast" to the organic activity. Further, the activity of reason is *in* self-consciousness. Accordingly, self-consciousness is that which stands over against the totality of emerging images, and self-consciousness, under the form of the I, is that which stands over against the particular individual and general emerging images (D236–37).

The image of the I arises codeterminately with the particular sense images of the world. The I emerges with and accompanies each image. The I has come to be to the extent that the sense image has come to be—the one accompanies the other.

As we have seen, the original state of consciousness is that of entangledness or confusion [*Verworrenheit*]. This is indeterminate consciousness filled with directionless activity of reason and undifferentiated sense impressions. Determinate consciousness arises out of this entangledness by means of the process of contrasting—a codetermination of the organic and intellectual functions. The result of this process entailed in determinate consciousness is the awareness of two kinds of forms: (1) the consciousness of things under the form of images and (2) self-consciousness under the form of the I.

The determinate I is the determination of self-consciousness that stands over against images—the objective consciousness of "things." This determinate I is the means Schleiermacher uses to "go behind it" to that which posited it. As we shall see, Schleiermacher will argue that this determinate I is posited by pure, unmediated self-consciousness—the pure I that refers to our very nature as our capacity as human beings to posit or locate and fix within ourselves that which we seek to know. This sheer capacity to posit is Schleiermacher's reference for the pure I, that is, unmediated self-consciousness. The determinate I, like the image, is that which is "the posited," that which is actually posited as a result of the mutually reciprocal activity of our organic and intellectual functions.

The world stirs the senses. This is the outside factor and is indeterminate. This world emerges in consciousness as a plurality of sense images. The I is stirred by the world; this is the inner factor. The I is the indeterminate unity that stands over against the indeterminate plurality which is the world (D237). Progressive determination produces conscious determinate images of the world and a conscious determinate I that accompanies those images.

The world arises as a unity upon which (1) a ground of separation is established and concomitantly, (2) the objective and subjective is discerned as a unity (not a duality) achieved through contrast. Furthermore, this contrast is a twofold contrast in which the activity from one side, when viewed from the other side is seen as predominantly receptive and passive.

Objective and Subjective Consciousness

Objective consciousness is reason's altered activity brought on by that which is exterior to it. Objective consciousness, as such, is a description of our state of consciousness viewed from the perspective of the organic function as the active agent in consciousness. From this vantage point, "The Object [*Object*] is posited in consciousness as the ground of impression; . . . it effects [*wirkt*], and is thus what is predominantly active. . . (D237)."

The organic function, from this standpoint, is that which occasions reason. This occasion, however, is not thinking [*Denken*]. Rather, the occasioning is simply an Object [*Object*] unknown to reason. Thinking begins when reason "fixes" this occasioning. This fixed occasioning (that is, the affection) is now an object [*Gegenstand*]—a determined unity of conscious thought. Something unknown has become known.

An external Object has become known as a *Gegenstand* internal to us—a thought. From the vantage point of reason, something has emerged from nothing. Matter, according to Schleiermacher, is the true nonexistence [*Nichtsein*]; reason cannot know it on its own terms (D417).

The object of thought [*Gegenstand*] is the unity that reason has determined through locating a place for the Object in consciousness. By so doing, reason makes itself known [*sich verkündigt*] by means of that determinate unity (that is, the *Gegenstand*) (D388). For Schleiermacher, Object refers to the unknown external thing. This external being, however, is the ground of an occasioning in us (thus of an affection). The external Object and the internal *Gegenstand* have a kind of "blurry" edge. They meet at this edge. The way in which Schleiermacher delineates this meeting place will allow him to bridge the gap between thinking and being.

Gegenstand refers to the known and therefore internal awareness of the thing. This object, accordingly, is a determinate moment of consciousness. If this determinateness is removed, we have only the chaos of impressions (D388). According to Schleiermacher, "all actual determinate thinking" is enclosed in the meeting (that is, the coincidence [*Zusammentreffen*]) of the two functions (D388). Determinate thinking pertains to the concurrence of each function in the other.

Subjective consciousness is a description of consciousness from the standpoint of reason as the active agent determining our mental life. From this perspective, "The actual true ground of knowledge is the intellectual function, the external factor however, the occasioning [*Veranlassung*] in the becoming of knowledge, is the actual way

in which our organic function is affected from outside [*Afficirtsein*]"
(D174).

Schleiermacher can now define the genuine [*eigentliche*] form of
the contrast between objective and subjective consciousness as the
difference in direction from which consciousness is described. This
difference in direction is expressed by the activity of the subject and
the object as the two sides of being (D552n).

From the vantage point of the organic function, the Object is the
active agent (D237). This Object is the real. It is nature, being, the
world. If the Object, however, is described as passive, it is the ideal.
It is part of the totality of our ideas about the world. The world is
never directly known by reason. External being is not present in
thinking in a direct and unmediated way. External being is present
only as the process of thinking about being. Accordingly,

> the world is also, although in a subordinate sense, tran-
> scendental . . . namely, in so far as the organic [world] can-
> not be given to us not ever anywhere [*nie und nirgend*], not
> even in the infinite process of the combining [*Zusammen-
> fassung*] of all experience, but is always given to us only as
> it is thought (D432–33).

The identity of the real and the ideal is our concept of the Object.
The concept of the Object is the common referent for the contrasted
standpoints of our intellectual and organic functions. Concerning
this, Schleiermacher states:

> We now wish to name that which constitutes the activity of
> the Object the **real**; and that which constitutes the passivity
> of the Object the **ideal.** The identity of the two is the con-
> cept of the Object. Here, however, the ideal is the activity
> and the real is the passivity (D553n).

A description of the world exclusively from the standpoint of
either the real or ideal is therefore inadequate. An adequate
description of the world must describe the world as both ideal and
real, active and passive in our process of cognition. The world
determines us and we determine what we call the world. A complete description of the thinking subject must thereby include the
subject as both an active and a passive agent.

Concepts and Judgments

Schleiermacher can now define what he means by a judgment, also what he means by the beginning and completion of a concept. The process of determination of images brings forth plurality—the untangling of the manifold of impressions with reference to the "thing" separated out from it.

Judgments begin with the determination given to the intellectual function by the organic function (D466), thus by affections yielded by the organic function. They begin where the concept has already been established. They are, in this way, closer to the organic function. They are the source of images in the concept (D410). Judgments thereby posit determinate, organic affections.

For Schleiermacher, judgments originally depend on the organic affections and therefore presuppose something externally given (D467). Judgments pertain to the intensive aspect of the process of concept formation, because they are what enables the fullness of the concept. They untangle the manifold of impressions that is already contained within or leads to the concept. They refer to the "sensible side" of the concept. This sensible aspect is the "image" or "schema" of the concept (D209). The judgment is the way in which the organic affections become "fixed" in consciousness [*Fixurtwerden*].

The image or schema is that within the concept which corresponds to the organic affections. Only when the image and the place posited by reason in consciousness correspond does an actual concept (image and place) emerge in consciousness (D207n). Accordingly, each judgment is a descent from the original "fullness"; something has been brought forth into determination. Judgments, in this way, bring clarification or definition to the first beginning of the concept (D497n). They untangle the chaotic manifold that lies in the initial formation of the concept.

Judgments complete or perfect the initial concept by means of a series of propositions that create an internally harmonious, general thought. The chaotic manifold that lies in the beginning of the concept is "resolved" [*aufgelöst*] into a determinate plurality of propositions (D497n). Reason, as this disentangling, resolving activity, is now the dominant activity in the determination of our organic affections. This activity is *a posteriori*; it is dependent on affections and presupposes something already given. This area of thinking as such pertains to empirical thinking, as this is manifest along with speculative knowing in natural science and history (D467). Such thinking concerns the real, the concept posited as an individual in the fullness of time and space (D468). Judgments are the form in which the organic function in our mental life is expressed in actual thinking.

Concepts, on the other hand, are *a priori*. They begin with the original impulse of reason. When this original impulse dominates our consciousness, speculative knowing occurs (D467). This process of knowing emerges from the inner impulse of reason to know that which is beyond it. Its original mode of expression is the formation of the concept (D467).

Determinate sense impressions, as we have seen, are brought about by the determining activity of reason. This determining activity of reason is judgment. Propositions about something have been posited. Schleiermacher calls that which has been separated out by this activity of reason "the separated" [*das gesonderte*] (D495). This is the posited agent in thinking. It is a thought about an organic agent in relationship to its place in intellection (that is, a concept). It is a cognized organic affection, a determinate image. This is Schleiermacher's definition of perception (D392–93).

Perception is actual thinking that is dominated by the activity of the organic function. Here, our thinking is actively determined by our senses; reason simply brings determinate form to the affections it has received—its activity is directed by the impulses of our organic affections. These affections are the posited agent. The activity of reason that brought about this posited agent is "that of positing" [*die Sezung*].

"Positing" is the original activity of reason; this activity posits, locates, fixes a group of sense impressions. This activity, as we have seen, marks the beginning of the concept. Schleiermacher refers to such thinking as "thinking in the narrow sense." From this standpoint, reason is the active agent in thinking. Reason takes the lead. We think [*Denken*] because we want to know something [*Denkenwollen*]. Our will to know [*Denkenwollen*] is that which lets us open our senses so that we can form concepts about the world (D392–93).

Schleiermacher notes that this process of positing by reason that he describes is very different from that described by Fichte, which begins not with an actual organic agent (that is, organic affections) but with hypothesis (D495) (that is, the artifice of thought). Accordingly, for Schleiermacher, Fichte succeeds only in canceling rather than combining thought in a shared, nonindividualistic way

(D495). Thought is combined and validated only when *both* reason and our organic affections are involved in the process of conceptualization. This is the master key to Schleiermacher's epistemology of being. The way in which we know is not merely the mental activity of reason, it is also the organic activity of our mental life as affected by the world.

One determining ground of our impressions, as we have seen, is internal to consciousness. This ground is the "place" of intellection (D496n–97n). The content of this intellectual place, from the vantage point of the organic function, is a "fixed" [*stätig*] concept, one that is entirely determinate (D402). This fullness is the extensive side of thinking (D496). This fullness is thinking in its most general form. Schleiermacher calls this place the beginning of the concept.

The completion of the concept is the process of defining or clarifying this fullness (D497). This is achieved by determining particularity and is the intensive side of thinking (D497n). Something is separated out of the concept and determined in relationship to it. Each determination thereby determines something that the manifold is not. Each articulation of this process is a proposition. Each proposition consists of a subject and predicate.

Subjects and predicates pertain to the way in which we think about things. The predicate refers to that which has been separated out—the subject. The predicate, as such, in the process of determining the subject, negates [*nigirt*] the manifold from which the subject was separated (D496). Schleiermacher identifies this process of predicating the subject as that of positing by means of a contrast [*das ist eine Entgegensezung*] (D496n) that is not a simple negation. Rather, two different things [*zweierlei*] are posited that reciprocally exclude each other (D495n). The subject at one and the same time is positively determined and also determined as that which the manifold is not.

Schleiermacher refers to the active determining ground of this manifold of impressions as external being. This ground extends beyond the immediate grasp of reason. External being is expressed in consciousness through the organic affections. Reason, as such, does not create external being. Reason simply determines external being by means of positing contrast, positing separation within it. Determinations of external being consist of the selection by reason of a group of sensible impressions. This group of impressions, from the organic perspective, is an image—the schema of the concept.

Furthermore, because reason can be conscious only of that in which it posits itself, that of which it is conscious must be something that was separable—could be separated into determinable parts by intellection (D236). Accordingly, that which is separable and that which separates must emerge into consciousness together (D236), because without the separable, separation and determination could not take place.

Schleiermacher can now conclude that all actual thinking is the separation of something from the manifold of impressions and the determining of that something through contrasting it with that manifold. Accordingly, all actual thinking is positing by means of separation and contrast [*Sonderung und Entgegensezung*] (D496n). The organic function ushers in [*bringt*] the entangled manifold, and the intellectual function brings forth [*bringt*] determination and separation and as such simultaneously posits unity and contrast [*also Einheitsezung, zugleich aber auch Gegensezung*] (D495).

The act of separating [*das Sondern*] is in this way always at the same time the act of positing something by means of contrast. That which is separated as two and that which is determined as one are both the work of the intellectual function. From the standpoint of the intellectual function, 'positing through contrast' does not mean that something is posited and something else is simply negated. Rather, as was stated above, this means that two very different kinds of things [*zweierlei*] are posited that reciprocally exclude each other (D495n).

The Limits of Determinate Thinking

Schleiermacher can now establish the limits of determinate thinking by simply removing the very possibility of determinability from the manifold of impressions. By so doing, he arrives at the limit of thinking from the organic perspective. Schleiermacher characterizes this limit as "chaos," because reason can neither "fix" it by means of properties nor engender a sensible image from it (D389). This limit is the possible beginning of thinking from the organic side. It is not actual thinking; it is simply organic affection, without which determinate thinking cannot take place.

This state can also be characterized as not-affection [*Nicht-affection*], because it is that which is indeterminable by reason. Schleiermacher characterizes this as the indifference established within one pole of the bipolarity entailed in thinking. He refers to this as the indifference of affection and not-affection (D389). From this indifference, no determinate thought can emerge into consciousness. This is sheer indeterminate being, the limit of thinking. This limit is not thinking.

The limit of thinking, from the intellectual perspective, is thinking without the possibility of being organically affected (D389). Thinking, without organic affection (that is, its contrast) is sheerly thinking contrast without actual contrast. Schleiermacher characterizes this limit to the intellectual function as the indifference of contrast and not-contrast [Nichtgegensaz] (D389). This limit simply indicates the possible beginning of thinking from the intellectual side. The very possibility of its being organically affected has been removed. Thus, in this way it is sheer being—being without the ability to act [Thun]. This limit of thinking is the sheer will without the ability to bring about that which is intended—determinate thinking.

All actual thinking consists of the unity of the organic and intellectual functions in their mutual turning to our organic affections (D498n). This is Schleiermacher's master key. All actual [wirkliche] thinking is dependent upon [bedingt durch] the codeterminate, contrasting relationship of the organic and intellectual functions (D494).

❖ ❖ ❖

Schleiermacher now has established the vocabulary necessary to redefine Kant's ethical subject and is able to divide Kant's subject into active reason and passive reason. In other words, Schleiermacher can examine the intellectual pole of thinking with regard to the two activities that he has defined as constitutive of reason. Reason, on the one hand, is instigated by the will to think determinately about the world. Reason, on the other hand, is an actual efficacious activity of thinking with reference to our organic nature as it is affected by the natural world.

Schleiermacher redefines Kant's ethical subject by refining the meaning of the organic and intellectual functions in thinking. He does this by making a distinction between thinking that is unmediated by external being [Denkenwollen] and thinking that is combined with external being [Denken]. He identifies the former as the will to think. When conceived by itself this is sheer volition without the ability to effectuate its will in the world. The latter is Denken, which is actual thinking, thinking that brings about that which it intends. Schleiermacher's distinction between these two forms of activity of reason allows him to establish the contrast between thinking and (external) being in a more precise manner than by simply referring to thinking and external being in general (D425).

Denkenwollen vs. Denken:
The Will to Think vs. Actual Thinking

Willing to think [*Denkenwollen*] can now be thought of as an aspect of reason, that which strictly pertains to the intellectual function in thinking. Thinking incorporates the organic function because it involves the organic affections; it is not sheer intellection. Both functions, however, pertain to reason. Schleiermacher can now refer to *Denkenwollen* itself as thinking without the direct influence of external being. *Denken*, on the other hand, is thinking directly influenced by external being. *Thinking* [*Denken*], in this scheme, involves the principle of combining that allows thinking to interact with (external) being (D425). *Thinking*, when contrasted with willing to think [*Denkenwollen*], can be regarded as itself a form of being. *Denkenwollen* is devoid of being by way of organic affections, whereas *Denken* is thinking combined with being by way of organic affections.

Denkenwollen, as an activity of the intellectual function, pertains solely to the activity of reason. As such, *Denkenwollen* simply represents reason's will to form particular sets of concepts. Whereas *Denken* requires empirical thinking.

Schleiermacher wants to find the basis of the transition in thinking from the will to think to actual thinking. That there is such a transition is unquestioned by Schleiermacher. He does not question the human experience of the continuity and interdependency of life for three basic reasons.

First, the concurrency [*Gemeinschaftlichkeit*] of being is expressed in the contrast of cause and effect, in which no thing is a cause simply by means of its own agency alone; rather, everything is in tandem. For instance, the fact that the fruit of the plant is in bloom at the present time has not occurred simply through the nature of the plant but also because of atmospheric conditions in relationship to the plant (D419).

Second, our basic ethical standpoint is that our will can in fact effectuate change. This standpoint presupposes a transition from mere possibility to actuality (D425). Third, we deem ourselves to be essentially volitional agents in that we will to have an effect on that which is other than ourselves (D425).

Schleiermacher has now arrived at the very heart of Kant's second *Critique*: reason's practical ability to effectuate action in the natural world solely through volitional activity. What is the means by which reason brings about this efficacy? Schleiermacher, as we saw in chapter one, believes that Kant could not answer the question based on his delineation of the ethical subject. Schleiermacher now begins the delineation of his own answer to this question by first establishing the ethical subject as entailing not one but two activities of reason. Schleiermacher, based on this method of distinguishing our two functions in thinking, can now refer to the ethical subject as follows.

The Ethical Subject

In part, the ethical subject pertains to the progressive determination by another of our affections by reason (D553n). The ethical subject is the activity of reason determining, by means of its own active agency, the world in which it lives. This subject is unrestrained by organic affections in the determination of its activity. It is "a constancy of free movement" (D553n).

The Physical Subject

Schleiermacher defines the physical subject by means of this same analysis. Our being, as that which is being combined into a determinate activity by the world, is the "physical subject" (D553n). The physical subject pertains to the self in its "vital co-existence" [*lebendigen Zusammensein*] with the entirety of posited individual being (D553n). In this aspect, the subject does not determine but rather is determined by another. Its consciousness is passive, receptive.

Schleiermacher's Three-fold Strategy

Schleiermacher's overall account of the self is much fuller and more complex than what has been abstracted. Now, however, it may be asked with respect to what has been singled out here: What has Schleiermacher done? First, he has established the ethical subject as the subject that is actively related to its object (*Gegenstand*) and the object's determining ground (*Object*). Second, the ethical subject, in this way, is the subject that expresses the principle of reason's activity of combining organic affections. As this active determining ground of being, reason is *thinking* [*Denken*]. Third, Schleiermacher has also established that an *adequate* description of the ethical subject must include a description of this ethical subject as a physical subject. The physical subject's activity of reason is that of actually participating in vital co-existence with other being. As strictly *Denkenwollen*, reason would be unable without the prior activity of thinking to activate itself in the world. In action, the two are reciprocally interdependent.

Schleiermacher's Master Key

Schleiermacher has now made it possible to describe the subject's activity of reason as interactively physical and ethical. In this way, the world is the object that either determines or is determined by the subject. This is Schleiermacher's master key. According to Schleiermacher, subject and object separate being into an inner and an outer factor (D552n). This separation rests upon the condition of the opened and filled senses.

Subject and object have a contrastive relationship to the senses and thereby to each other. Accordingly, a description of one as active means that the other must be described as passive. If, for instance, the subject is described as active, then the object must be described as passive. The subject, however, is both active and passive in determinate consciousness. So, too, is the object. Thus, the relationship between subject and object is that of a "two-fold contrast" (D238). Subject and object must each be described as active and passive in order to have an adequate description of each. Accordingly, the ethical subject is only a partial description of reason's activity. The physical subject is the other side of the ethical subject and must be taken into account if the subject's activity of reason is to be adequately described. The unity of the subject thus entails a description of the subject as the unity of reason as both active and passive.

Schleiermacher now wants to find the basis of the transition in thinking from the will to think to actual thinking (and vice versa). Schleiermacher does not question that there is such a transition; he simply wants to explain it. Using a model of the transition in reason from sheer volition to actual efficacious thinking, Schleiermacher now seeks the source of this transition. His master key tells him that to unlock the answer to this question, he must look to reason's other: organic being.

Since the ethical and physical subject both pertain to the two forms of thinking (D424), Schleiermacher now seeks a way of ascertaining the nature of this transition, not from the standpoint of thinking but from the standpoint of our organic nature as part of the natural world of being. Schleiermacher undertakes this search because he knows that when *Denken* is dominant, reason is actively combining being. Here, reason is the predominant activity.

Kant, Beck, and Fichte Revisited

What makes this transition from being to thinking possible? Schleiermacher has now arrived at the core of Kant's, Beck's, and Fichte's concern, that is, the search for the link between active and passive thinking. To answer this question, Schleiermacher turns to the human being, not simply as a bodiless mind—the logical subject—but as the unity of mind and body, thinking and being. We, as human beings, Schleiermacher insists, are the actual unity of thinking and organic agency. How is it that we are both as one unity? To answer this question, Schleiermacher begins his search for the place of transition in our being as organic agents that is the organic expression of the transition point in thinking between *Denken* and *Denkenwollen*. This search, as we shall see in chapter four, leads Schleiermacher to his solution to the problem of the gap in Kant's critical philosophy.

CHAPTER FOUR

Schleiermacher's Original Insight

Schleiermacher's careful analysis of the transition between *Denkenwollen* and *Denken* in the ethical subject allowed him to narrow his focus to the transition point that these two modalities of reason have in common. The common point, which for Schleiermacher became the site of the unchanging transcendental ground of ever-shifting determinate thought, gave him his own counterpart to Fichte's requisite "highest standpoint." In this chapter, I shall argue that the standpoint that Schleiermacher devised to discern this transition point is the little-understood source of his recognition today as the father of modern Protestant theology.[1] Simply stated, I believe that the basis of Schleiermacher's fame is founded, in part, on the way in which he solved the problem of the gap in Kant's theory of self.

The highest principle of Kant's critical philosophy, the transcendental unity of apperception, from the perspective of Schleiermacher's highest standpoint, became the point of transition, "the indifference point" between *Denken* and *Denkenwollen*. Self-consciousness, in Schleiermacher's work, became the experience of a particular person in a particular place. The identity of this particular self, however, rests on its immediate awareness of itself as inextricably one with the world. This certainty of the self's oneness with nature was for Schleiermacher the sanctioning ground of the ongoing identity of the self in its individuated moments of objective consciousness.

As we saw in chapter three, Schleiermacher reconfigured Kant's ethical self as *both* an active and a receptive agent in the natural world. As both active and receptive, the self is both subject (that which acts) and object (that which is acted upon). An adequate delineation of the self is thus a description of the self as both subject and object and its object as both subject and object. Each side must be described as both active and passive. Accordingly, there is an ongoing transition from activity to passivity and back again.

Schleiermacher was clear about the task at hand: he had to delineate the non-sensate, noncognizable point of transition in thinking without reducing it to thought. His *Dialektik* served this purpose. All knowing, Schleiermacher suggested, is thinking; but which thinking is knowing (D315)? His *Dialektik* provided his answer to this question, because it was, for him, a product of the very principles entailed in all thinking that wills to know [*Wissenwollen*]. The true major concern of his *Dialektik* is to establish and delineate the structure of the transcendental ground of knowing (D503n). To do this, he must delineate the relationship of the two functions of thinking, and the relationship of thinking to being. He must then demonstrate that the coincidence of these two relationships is the transition point from one determinate moment of consciousness to the next.

As we saw in chapter three, the intellectual and organic functions of thinking pertain to knowledge as (1) *Wissenwollen*, the will to know, which presupposes all determinate thinking, and (2) *Werden des Wissen*, the becoming of knowing, which is the principle entailed in determinate thinking by means of which the will to know is realized (D174). All actual [*wirkliche*] thinking is dependent upon the codeterminate, contrasting relationship of these two functions. This, in essence, is Schleiermacher's master key that allowed him to escape the perpetual circle of Kant's theory of self-consciousness.

The mutual codetermination of these two functions of the same subject and object makes the contrast between subject and object a double contrast (D238) when considered in relation to the first affection—the opening and filling of the sense organs. Both subject and object must be described as active and passive in this relationship. As we shall see, the ideas 'God' and 'World' became for Schleiermacher the highest expression in determinate thinking of this mutually reciprocal and codeterminate relationship.

Knowing, according to Schleiermacher, pertains to the two distinct but inseparable ideas ('God' and 'World'). He presented his *Dialektik* as the product of the principles entailed in the relationship of these two ideas (D173). His investigation of these two inseparable ideas entailed an intricate study of (1) the way in which we think about being, and (2) the way in which we arrive at knowledge.

In the work that follows, I will continue the explication begun in chapter three of the way Schleiermacher believes that we think about being. The present discussion will enable us to understand why Schleiermacher believed that all such discussions lead to "God-consciousness." Here, we will discover the core of Schleiermacher's own original insight into Kant's theory of the self.

The Point of Indifference

Schleiermacher identified our capacity to think, stripped of all determinate thinking. He called this capacity "that which remains left over" when we are not actually thinking about something (D429). As we saw in chapter three, Schleiermacher refined his discussion of the two operations referred to as the intellectual function and the organic function in thinking (D492–95) into thinking combined with and thus affected by being [*Denken*] and thinking unaffected by being [*Wollen*]. In fact, in all willing "our being is posited in things in our own manner" (D429). Both *Wollen* and *Denken*, then, refer to the activity of reason and as such became a more precise analysis of the contrasts entailed in the intellectual function in thinking as it shifts from an active to a passive (receptive) activity and back again. This shift within the intellectual function also means that a shift has gone on in the organic function, because the two are reciprocally codeterminate. Schleiermacher now argues that when thinking shifts from one determinate moment of consciousness to the next, neither function is determining a moment of consciousness during the transition.

Rather, in the transition between two determinate moments of consciousness, one thought has come to an end and another thought is about to begin. The transition is the coincidence of this end and new beginning, which has not yet begun. Accordingly, in the transition, no thinking is going on. This shift, as such, is not a determinate moment of thinking but is between two such moments (D429). Schleiermacher refers to this intermediate point as the "nullpoint" [*Nullpunkt*] (D429) or "point of indifference" [*Indifferenzpunkt*] (D532n), which is the having-ceased of one function and the not-yet-having-begun of the other function (524n). The "indifference point" is the border that both functions have in common.

The precise way in which Schleiermacher established this "indifference point" is graphically illustrated in one of his 1822 lectures. In this lecture, Schleiermacher begins his investigation of the means of transition in ourselves from one moment of determinate consciousness to the next by first establishing *the self as the means of the transition between the two functions of thinking*. Schleiermacher does this by asking us to regard life as a series of relative, antithetical transitions from *Denken* to *Wollen* and back again (D428–29).

What is the means of these transitions in us as the organic agent—the being—in which this transition takes place? This *means*, Schleiermacher suggests, must be the same for both *Denken* and *Wollen*. Otherwise, there could not be a crossing over, a transition. Schleiermacher concludes that this transition is the "common border" which is found in "the positing" [*das sezende*] modality of our own being.

To understand his answer, we must first determine what Schleiermacher is referring to as our positing modality. As we shall see, this modality is itself not the actual activity of positing. Rather, it is *that which makes possible the activity of positing*; it is that in which we are involved as organic beings who think (D396). Schleiermacher arrives at his characterization of this most basic human modality in the following way.

First, Schleiermacher identifies thinking [*Denken*] as the activity of external being determining our consciousness of things. Here, thinking is combined with being and is given its "stimulus" by that which is external to it. This determination of things, however, is posited in us "in our own manner" [*auf unsre Weise*]—according to our own modality as human beings who think (D396).[2] In other words, human beings think "in our own manner" in as much as our nature differs in its modalities from those of other species. Even though external being is the determining ground of our consciousness of things from the perspective of the organic function, the *way* in which we are conscious of this pertains solely to our own human mode of awareness. This mode of awareness pertains to ourselves (*homo sapiens*) and to our unique position as a particular determination of a particular self (the determinate *I*). 'Our manner', as such, is distinct from the external determining ground (the sensate world) of our consciousness.

Schleiermacher refers to this way of ours of being aware of that which affects us from outside, as one of our modalities. Specifically, that modality is our capacity to posit. This positing capacity [*das sezende*] is a description of the pure *I*. Positing, as we saw in chapter three, is our way of knowing by means of 'placing' (or 'fixing') before our mind's eye so that something becomes known. That which we place, we know. This is the way in which something is "fixed" in consciousness. For us, to place in us is to know. That which we place in our awareness from the organic perspective is external being as received via sense impressions. This placing marks the place in consciousness of our awareness of things. *Denken*, as we saw in chapter three, quite literally re-presents the world. It is the expression of the external determining ground of our organic function in thinking.

Second, Schleiermacher identifies *Wollen* as the sheer activity of reason, which he characterizes as internal being (that is, reasoning) determining our consciousness of things. From this perspective, we place our being into the objects of consciousness. In other words, we know by means of inserting reason into that which we seek to know (that is, the manifold of sense impressions). Through this insertion/separation we determine that which we know. By so doing, we place our (internal) being into objects. *Wollen*, as we saw in chapter three, pertains solely to the activity of reason as the "according reality to what we will."

Third, Schleiermacher now states that these two different activities of reason (*Wollen* and *Denken*) are coterminus, in that in so far as the (organic) being of things is not posited in us, our being (reason) will be posited in things. Schleiermacher now looks for the terminus of both. What is it that both have in common? He concludes that the common point is our modality of positing. This modality refers neither to the internal agency of reason nor to the external agency of organic being in objective consciousness. Whether we are positing our being in things or whether exterior being is positing things in us, our modality is the way in which this positing activity and passivity (receptivity) takes place in us. This modality is itself not an actual act of positing. Rather, it is that which makes both forms of positing possible and is that which the two have in common.

The Common Border

Schleiermacher now designates the indifference point as the "common border" which is in us as organic agents who *can* think. In other words, whether we *are* thinking or not we remain organic agents who have the capacity to think and are always part of the organic world. Schleiermacher, by making this distinction between the capacity to think and actual thinking, can now investigate the self, which is sheerly the capacity to think, as the means of transition for thinking. This sheer capacity, Schleiermacher will argue, is not thinking, but the *self* that thinks and remains when thinking has *ceased*. This self (the pure I) is the means that makes possible the shift in our thinking from one determinate moment of consciousness to the next. This pure I is not thinking but the organic agency that makes thinking possible. Schleiermacher identifies this place of transition in thinking as our own subjective modality that presupposes all objective consciousness (D429).

This place is not our actual activity of thinking; it is not a moment of consciousness. Accordingly, it is not a determinate I. Rather, it is our very *capacity* to be conscious and to think. This very capacity to posit is that which is left over when we strip the activity of positing from its actual positing activity. This indifference point between two determinate moments of consciousness is located in the self and is in fact the self's location as thinking's continuity.

Schleiermacher has now identified a "point" or "place" in ourselves as organic agents that both forms of thinking have in common, but that is not itself a part of either form of thinking. This modality is "that which is left over." This place of transition for thinking is not thinking per se, but is that which makes thinking possible.

It is important to note here that Schleiermacher has now gone beyond Fichte's notion of the *I* by identifying the *I* that is distinct from both the intellectual and organic functions in thinking. Fichte conceived of the *I* as pure thinking. Such a notion in Schleiermacher's scheme is revealed to be one-sided; it is sheerly activity of reason, which is only one of two operations in the formation of a concept. Schleiermacher, by identifying an I distinct from the two forms of thinking, can now argue that this (pure) I is distinct from the operations of thinking and is that which is left over when thinking has ceased in its transition from one determinate moment of thinking to the next and that always accompanies both.

Schleiermacher now designates this ever-accompanying feature as that which is in us as organic agents. It is the means of transition that makes possible the shift in our thinking from one determinate moment of consciousness to the next; it is that which is in between thinking. This is our self as that which makes possible our thinking as both an active and a passive (receptive) agent in the natural world. This is the organic I.

In an 1831 lecture, Schleiermacher identifies this same noncognitive, organic I in the following way. Schleiermacher suggests that as a being that senses, we are agents that receive what external being expresses as its own reality and concomitantly receive according to our own modalities. External being is posited in us by means of what is possible within our own nature. Using Fichtean language, Schleiermacher characterizes this positing of external being in us as the return of ourselves to ourselves [*in sich zurüchgehen*]. We are given back to or return to ourselves as that which is being received. This is the self as passive agent in the formation of concepts. Schleiermacher characterizes our spontaneous impulse of reason, again using Fichtean language, as the self going out of itself [*aus sich herausgehen*]. Here the self is the active agent that seeks that which it wishes to know. This is the volitional agency of thinking. Schleiermacher refers to that which is left over (and accordingly is not these two activities of thinking) as the point of indifference (D532n).

This point of indifference between the two moments is located in the self, but not as the one or the other moment. Rather, this in-between point is the having-just-come-to-an-end of the self going out of itself and the not-yet-having-begun of the self going back to itself. Schleiermacher, as mentioned above, uses the term *indifference point* to characterize this transition from one function of thinking to the other (D532n). This transition is the having-ceased of one function and the yet-not-having-begun of the other (D524n).[3] At this 'indifference point', neither of the two functions of thinking predominates. This is the border which both functions have in common.

The Means of Transition

Schleiermacher has now arrived at the place which he sought; he has found the common border between *Denken* and *Wollen*. He can now investigate this common border in order to identify the 'link' between thinking and (organic) being. Here he will find the 'missing link' that eluded Kant, Beck, and Fichte. This link, because it is the 'border,' is neither one nor the other function of thinking. Rather, it is that which makes possible the transition from one function to the other.

This common border between two determinate moments of consciousness is, for Schleiermacher, the referent for that which Kant called the transcendental presupposition of knowledge. This border is Schleiermacher's counterpart to the synthetic unity of apperception that Kant's critical philosophy presupposes rather than reveals. The means of transition [*der Übergang*], for Schleiermacher, is that which both forms of thinking have in common. Without this common border, no thinking is possible. Schleiermacher concludes that the act of crossing over [*Der Übergehen*] = the presupposition of all determinate thinking (D509).

The presupposition is that (organic) being and thinking cross over into each other by means of their common border (D509n). Without this presupposition, there can be no development of thought or any consciousness of such development.[4] This presupposition is based, in turn, on the assumption that the totality of thinking corresponds to and is identical to the totality of things (D497n). This is a transcendental presupposition, and for two reasons: first, objective thinking cannot demonstrate this correspondence but always only presupposes it; and second, the ground of thinking is not, itself, thinking (D504).

Kant's transcendental principle of knowledge, the synthetic unity of apperception, no longer refers to the act of combining sense impressions. In Schleiermacher's lexicon, this principle refers to the *transition* that makes all such combining possible. Schleiermacher can now ask: "What does this presupposition mean?" His answer gives him a basic map to the link that binds thinking to the world.

According to Schleiermacher, we assume, a priori, that our act of thinking about something and that which we are thinking are necessarily linked by a common border. This common border specifies the area in which the link between thinking and its objects can be found. Schleiermacher claims that anyone who denies this presupposition cannot will to know (D509n). Without such a presupposition, Schleiermacher argues, we cannot presume that we know even that which we think. This is the way in which Schleiermacher addresses the *crise pyrrhonienne*,[5] what Schleiermacher terms the "positive skepticism" (D548n) of his day, which he wishes to dispel. He wants to demonstrate the rectitude in presupposing the identity of the *totality* of the being given to us with the system of concepts lying in the intellect [*Intelligenz*] (D548n).[6] To do this, he must investigate the link that binds one to the other. This link is the boundary shared by both forms of thinking.

Schleiermacher's correspondence theory of truth has a 'soft' edge. He cannot claim that we actually know that our thoughts and the sensate world to which they refer correspond or that they cohere. Such knowledge is possible only after the totality of all possible ways of thinking about the sensate world have in fact been thought. Rather, Schleiermacher wishes to explain why we believe that there is a correspondence between thinking and being. He argues that without such a presupposition we cannot even claim that we know our own thoughts. This claim, Schleiermacher argues, is absurd because the fact that we claim these thoughts as "mine" already acknowledges that which we seek to deny—that we believe that thinking (subject) and that which is thought (object) are one. This unity is expressed as "my" thought. The object is acknowledged to be distinct from the self that claims it as "mine."

The presupposition that external "things" and internal objective thinking cohere, Schleiermacher concludes, is the transcendental ground of knowledge as it pertains to objective thinking. Writes Schleiermacher, "What lies at the ground of thinking? Nothing other than the presupposition that **the totality of the beginning of concepts and the totality of things** correspond to one another, i.e., are identical" (D497n).

This totality, Schleiermacher argues, is the unity of all being and all thinking as one. As we saw in chapter three, this totality, from the standpoint of objective consciousness, is the manifold of impressions that both forms of thinking codetermine. Schleiermacher must now demonstrate that this presupposition is more than a mere presupposition. He must delineate the way in which we are actually aware of this totality and unity of (organic) being and thinking. Only then will he be able to demonstrate the actual link between mind and body that eluded Kant. To do this, Schleiermacher must investigate the content of the border of the two forms of thinking from the standpoints of both objective consciousness and subjective consciousness.

Schleiermacher knows that the unity of thinking and being cannot be objectively known, because such a knowledge would presuppose that *all possible being and thinking have occurred.* Accordingly, the presupposition of this unity is a transcendental presupposition. Objective (that is, "narrow") thinking simply presupposes the fact (rather than the already-having-occurred actuality) of this unity. Accordingly, this presupposition is that upon which all thinking is based. The actual referent for this presupposition, however, is not itself thinking.

Schleiermacher must now undertake an investigation of the noncognizable ground of thinking. He will do this by exploring the border, the common point that the two functions share but that is not itself an actual moment of thinking. Acknowledging the difficulty of such a task, he concedes that the task would be impossible if he began this investigation from the standpoint of thinking.

Using an insight gained from his study of Fichte's work, Schleiermacher now seeks to establish a transcendental standpoint that will enable him to be aware of thinking's limit without reducing this limit to a thought. Schleiermacher describes his transcendental standpoint from two perspectives, that of objective and subjective consciousness. From the standpoint of objective consciousness, he calls this transcendental standpoint "unmediated intuition" [Anschauung].

Anschauung: Object-less Awareness

According to Schleiermacher, Anschauung (unmediated or immediate intuition) consists of the organic and intellectual functions of thinking at their point of indifference (D532n). For Schleiermacher, this point of indifference, as we have seen, is the actual point of transition by means of which thinking shifts from one determinate moment of consciousness to the next. This shift is itself not an actual moment of objective consciousness.

In an actual moment of objective consciousness, we are conscious of something, but in Anschauung Schleiermacher believes that we are conscious of nothing (524n), no-thing. Schleiermacher identifies this state as self-consciousness (as described from the objective standpoint of thinking). According to Schleiermacher, "Self-consciousness, viewed apart from all determined content, is nothing other than consciousness of the oneness and the belonging together [Zusammengehörigkeit] of the two functions" (D414).

This consciousness has no actual content. Rather, our mind is in the state of the cessation of thinking, or that which Schleiermacher refers to as the state of "canceled thinking." I will refer to this state as 'object-less awareness' because this state of objective consciousness is empty of thought; it is object-less. Schleiermacher, as we have seen, defines objective consciousness as consciousness that is aware of an object. Accordingly, *Anschauung* is objective-consciousness without an object that is, object-less awareness. In this state, neither concepts nor judgments occur; our cognitive, mental life is still. Objective consciousness has reached its own nullpoint. This null-point, as we shall see, is Schleiermacher's equivalent to the gap that appears when Kant canceled reason so as to make room for faith. More importantly for our present discussion, this nullpoint is Schleiermacher's equivalent to the gap in Kant's theory of self-consciousness. Here, thinking has reached its limit and *is* its limit. This limit of thinking is the state of thinking as *Anschauung*, thought empty of all actual content. Consciousness of no-thing.

Our actual awareness [*Anschauung*] as this limit is not a presupposition but is an immediate state of our mind that is unknowable by means of either concepts or judgments. This state of mind, as such, is a transcendental standpoint; it is that which makes determinate thinking possible but is not itself thinking. It is a state of mind that is thinking's link to its next thought. This is an entirely different state of consciousness than that of thinking.

In trying to fathom such a state of mind, we might find it helpful to recall William James's attempt to delineate his own discovery of a state of mind different from "our normal waking consciousness" in his book *The Varieties of Religious Experience*, when he described the results of his own intake of nitrous oxide in order to stimulate his own state of mystic consciousness.[7] Writes James:

> One conclusion was forced upon my mind at that time, and my impression of its truth has ever since remained unshaken. It is that our normal waking consciousness, rational consciousness as we call it, is but one special type of consciousness, whilst all about it, parted from it by the filmiest of screens, there lie potential forms of consciousness entirely different. . . . Looking back on my own experiences, they all converge towards a kind of insight to which I cannot help ascribing some metaphysical significance. The keynote of it is invariably a reconciliation. It is as if the opposites of the world, whose contradictoriness and conflict make all our difficulties and troubles, were melted into a unity.[8]

This is a state of mind that can be affirmed only by one's own experience of unmediated awareness.

Gefühl: Subject-less Awareness

Schleiermacher can now ask himself: "What is it in ourselves as organic beings who think, that is the counterpart to *Anschauung*?' Schleiermacher's answer, but now considered from the standpoint of subjective rather than objective consciousness, is again self-consciousness. Schleiermacher calls this subjective transcendental standpoint "feeling" [*Gefühl*] (D429).

Gefühl, according to Schleiermacher, is not sensation [*Empfindung*]. Sensation pertains to the subjective personality (the determinate *I*) in a determinate moment of experience. A determinate moment of experience pertains to the organic affections (D429). Sensation is the not-one and not-the-other of the two functions. No positive, determinate expression arises from this. *Gefühl*, on the other hand, is the positive expression of the identity of our being. This identity, or unity, is the oneness [*Einheit*] of the *denkend wollenden* and the *wollend denkenden* (thinking willing and willing thinking) of being. The term *Gefühl* denotes the identity of *Denken* and *Wollen*—unmediated or immediate self-consciousness (D429).

Gefühl is the point of transition between and within each moment of determinate consciousness. It is the pure I's experience as the unity of being, as the conjunct of the oneness or unity of the two functions, which is the rising above or canceling [*Aufhebung*] of the contrasts that arise with these two functions.

Determinate consciousness, as we have seen, pertains to consciousness of something (D524). It is object-determined. As a transition, self-consciousness, from this standpoint, is "consciousness of null" [*Bewußtsein von Null*] (D524). It is consciousness that lies at the *Nullpunkt*; it is consciousness of the "point of indifference" between the two functions (D532). *Anschauung* is the awareness of this point of indifference of the two functions from the standpoint of objective consciousness. *Gefühl* is the awareness of this point of indifference by subjective consciousness from this nonthinking, organic standpoint.

Gefühl is the positive expression of the unity of our being. This consciousness is not an awareness of the I as something, but the unmediated and unreflected consciousness of the I's identity in two distinct moments of consciousness. *Gefühl* is the consciousness that *I* = *I* from one moment of consciousness to the next. It is the content by means of which the transition from one determinate moment of consciousness to the next is made and the identity of the I maintained (D524) as thinking shifts.

The actual content of the self in the transition point is not a specifically determinate state of the self. Here, the self is between two actual moments of determination. In this border point, all individuation has been canceled because thinking, which is the activity of determining "things," has been canceled. Accordingly, the self is not determined and is thus unbounded and limitless. Here thinking is not determining anything so that the self that is in any case part of the organic world is not seen to be distinct from the rest of the world. No determinate I emerges; rather the self is indistinguishable from the rest of life. Objectively, the *content* of this limitless self is null (D524). Here, "knowing" or rather, awareness, is without content. Thinking is aware of no-thing. This state of consciousness, as we have seen, is object-less. Self-consciousness, objectively described, is simply *Anschauung*.

Yet, subjectively, the content of this unbounded self is not simply null; it is not empty but full. The self, in this state, is "not a consciousness of something, but [consciousness] of the self. . . . [It is] self-consciousness" (D524). In this state, our consciousness of the indifference point between our two modes is *felt* in the identity of the two modes of thinking, the physical and the ethical (D528n). We *feel* the rupture in human consciousness; the cancellation of thinking. Simply stated, we do not think or even will the gap, we feel it. This is Schleiermacher's original insight.

A passage taken from his 1831 lectures provides us with a vivid indication of the way in which Schleiermacher believes that feeling is linked to thinking in particular. Here Schleiermacher suggests that the contrast [*Entgegensezung*] between the relationship of thinking and organic being in our two forms of thinking has its proper and actual [*eigentlichen*] place in that series of our consciousness where the change between both occurs and self-consciousness makes itself felt or asserts itself [*sich geltend macht*] in the identity of these two forms of thinking (D528n).[9]

The meaning of this passage must be unpacked. To do this, I will focus on two events referred to in this passage. One event is the shift or change [*Wechsel*] in thinking from one function to the other. The other event is the way in which self-consciousness "is authenticated" or is felt as the organic agency of the world.

The first event is the state of *Anschauung*. The second is that of *Gefühl*. Feeling is the way in which being is linked to thinking. Schleiermacher can make this claim because he has aligned *Gefühl* and *Anschauung* (D528n). He has aligned this shift or change

[*Wechsel*] in thinking from one function to the other with the way in which this shift is authenticated. From the standpoint of thinking, our immediate awareness of this shift in thinking is the state of *Anschauung*; it is the point of transition between two determinate moments of objective consciousness. From the standpoint of subjective consciousness, the immediate awareness of this shift in thinking is *Gefühl*. Both states refer to the place where thinking has been risen above, or canceled.

Gefühl, in Schleiermacher's scheme, coincides with the null-point of objective consciousness. The nullpoint is thus the gap in thinking that conceals the mind's link to being. The gap is the rupture, that is, the cancellation of thinking, that the self feels. Feeling is linked to thinking as thinking's orientation, the origination of thinking's attitude toward life, the source of thinking's frame of mind about life. In other words, in this respect *Gefühl* is the content of *Anschauung*'s frame of mind. Both content and form are unbounded. This is the subjective/objective state of sheer openness. Here, thinking is sheerly a mental standpoint, an attitude toward life. Accordingly, our awareness is object-less and so the mind simply abides and is the state of sheer openness.

In this state, it is as if thought has quite literally brinked the portal beyond itself, touched the limitless world, and is thus in the sheer state of contemplative, meditative awe born as a "view . . . so subtle and delicate that the understanding cannot grasp it."[10] Stripped of our ability to think or to act in this border place because thinking and action have been risen above or canceled, we simply are the feeling of our nonindividuated self as a part of the natural world. For Schleiermacher, this unbounded state is "the birth hour of everything living in religion."

According to Schleiermacher, this feeling of oneness with the world of being that fills and thereby directs our emptied mind is the state of certitude. I believe that it is not inappropriate to describe this state as the mind transfixed as engagement, wonder, or awe. Schleiermacher, however, is quite emphatic that this original state is not itself a religious experience. A feeling of certitude does emerge, but this feeling refers to the feeling of the fullness of life. This certitude is precisely a certitude regarding life (D529).

The self in this state is the feeling of life itself. To understand what Schleiermacher means by this, we must remember that Schleiermacher turned to our organic nature to find the means of transition that makes it possible for us to be an actual unity of thinking and being. Schleiermacher found that the "closest" [*nächste*] ground to the relationship of these two functions lies in us (D517n). In other words, "The immediate identity of being and thinking is, of course, given in ourselves." It is given immediately, as life itself. The more purely speculative thought becomes, the more does our immediate awareness of our life recede.

Stripped of our ability to think in this border place, because this is the point where thinking has been canceled, nevertheless we are still aware. Subjectively, this awareness is feeling. Here we simply are the feeling of our non-individuated self as part of the natural world. Here, the reality of the world is indistinguishable from our own reality as a non-individuated aspect of this world. We are not individuated, because thinking—which is the means by which we individuate—has been canceled. Thus, as a non-individuated part of the natural world, we are life, all of it. We are the world. We are the same life as all of life. We and the world are one. This is why Schleiermacher designates self-consciousness as consciousness of life, our own and all life, as one.

Gefühl can best be characterized as "subject-less awareness." I have derived the term "subject-less awareness" from Dieter Henrich's use of the term "subject-less knowing." In his essay "Fichte's Original Insight," Henrich characterized subject-less knowing as "a state of knowledge in which there is no knowing subject."[11] Henrich recognized the paradox of such a proposition. I believe that Henrich's discussion of this paradox is a fitting description of Schleiermacher's own effort to work his way back to this most basic principle of knowing and *the self*. According to Henrich,

> . . . it is certainly paradoxical to assume a state of knowledge in which there is no knowing subject. It seems clear that we can only speak of knowledge if we can also designate the agent who has knowledge. However, if the Self of the subject already has knowledge, then this allegedly self-evident principle cannot hold true without restriction. That is, if every item of knowledge really had a subject, then subject itself could not be an item of knowledge. Otherwise we would have to assume a subject of this subject and thus surrender to the infinite regress that Fichte had so feared. The idea of the Self would sink into the abyss. The paradox of subject-less knowing is preferable to that. If we take this paradox seriously, it is not astonishing that when we reach the central point, perhaps even the ground, of all knowing,

we can no longer find the structures familiar to us from the way we describe cognition of individual states of affairs or derivative insights. People who try to work out a philosophical theory of the Self must consider the possibility that forms of explication germane to the world must be given up when we make our way back to the basic principles.[12]

Henrich, as we saw in chapter two, acknowledges that Fichte's attempt to work his way back to a genuinely new philosophical theory of the self had failed. Schleiermacher, as we have seen, rejected Fichte's attempt, claiming that he did not make enough of the I. Fichte's I pertained to thinking but not to our organic agency as a part of the natural world. Schleiermacher, by contrast, established something akin to Henrich's subject-less "knowing" [Gefühl] as the subjective basis of self-identity in all determinate consciousness. I refer to this state as subject-less *awareness* so as to avoid confusing this state with *Wissen* (knowing), which Schleiermacher distinguished from feeling.[13]

This feeling is the embodiment of all life; it is life's awareness itself. *Gefühl* is unbounded corporeality, limitless organic-expressiveness. It is life-presence, the organic pulse, body-expression—the sheer embodied self that is the counterbalance to the [Kantian] 'I think'. This embodied self is subject-less because it is one, identified with the entire organic world; no-thing is distinct from this self. There is no subject; there is no object. This is the embodied self that Schleiermacher found in his effort to complete Kant's own one-sided theory of the self!

We must pause here a moment to reflect upon what Schleiermacher has done. He has aligned *Anschauung* and *Gefühl*, thereby making his transcendental standpoint the coincidence of thinking and organic being. By so doing, has he not then begged the question which he sought to answer by arbitrarily presupposing the alignment that he sought to demonstrate? I do not think that we must necessarily reach this conclusion, and for two basic reasons. First, in Schleiermacher's scheme he has not simply stated a presupposition but rather he has described an awareness, a sort of experience, or perhaps better put, an organic experiential content: his transcendental standpoint, the legacy bequeathed to him by Fichte. This awareness is the state of sheer unity of being with the mind framed as in repose. This description is Schleiermacher's explanation of our mental and physical certitude regarding of life, our own and that of the rest of the world. From this standpoint, Schleiermacher is engaged in sheer description. If it has a "ring of truth to it," I would suggest that it is because he has explained the way in which we actually live our daily lives (our experience of coherence between our thoughts and the sensate world) and during rare moments (for example, the "runner's high" or a special moment of lovemaking) are fully aware of this state because we are experiencing it as an altered state of consciousness linked to our feeling of limitless being.

We do not doubt that we are alive and as such that there is life. When we speculate about life, we are simply abstracting from the most basic facts of our ongoing experience of ourselves: that we are sentient moments of living experience. As Alfred North Whitehead has noted in his book *Science and the Modern World*,[14] we cannot think without abstractions from our experience of nature; the error is to mistake these abstractions as the concrete organic experiences they presuppose. Whitehead calls this error "the fallacy of misplaced concreteness."[15] Schleiermacher does not make this error and in fact has given us the description of an awareness that all abstraction presupposes. He has given us a way to affirm that which we never doubt, without positing the reference for this claim as a datum of empirical knowledge. We always have certitude regarding life as a lived moment of experience; Schleiermacher has descriptively delineated this awareness.

Second, Schleiermacher's alignment of our objective and subjective state is the core of his master key that allows him to break out of Kant's self ('the I think'), which was perpetually encased in its own thinking. Schleiermacher's claim that reason is an activity that both separates and combines in order to know necessitates that there is in fact something to be known, but this logical necessity does not mean that there is indeed really something distinct from the activity of reason. Schleiermacher's claim that there is such is based on his version of a correspondence theory of truth. He acknowledges that this theory is based on a presupposition. He never claims that this presupposition can be affirmed or denied by determinate thinking. Rather, he simply investigates what the actuality of this presupposition quite literally feels like. This actuality is *Anschauung* aligned with *Gefühl*. Schleiermacher never claims this alignment as a cognizable fact or a datum of sensible knowledge, such as a percept. If the *form* of his discussion is tautological, it is only because the content of the claim is a reciprocity that cannot be "stilled" except as the still-point itself—which for Schleiermacher is the highest standpoint of human nature itself.

The Source of Certitude

Schleiermacher now undertakes a line of reasoning that will lead him to something he calls "consciousness of God." As a philosopher, his referent for the term *God* pertains sheerly to the initial consciousness of the transition point that both cancels and unites thinking and being, as the source of the self's own identity. Schleiermacher, however, does not posit deity in any specific sense as this source. He cannot, because the transition point itself is not a determinate moment of experience. Accordingly, no positively determined claim can be made about its content. At this most basic level of human experience, Schleiermacher cannot make theistic claims.

As we have seen, Schleiermacher claims that our basic feeling regarding life takes place in the transition from one conscious experience to the next. During this transition, the "cancellation" of, or "rising above," of the self as the source of its own determination takes place as well. It is no longer its own determining agent because thinking has been canceled. According to Schleiermacher, the rupture in human consciousness is the symbolic indication of the hidden ground of our unity (D435). The gap is present because of the cancellation of the self as the agent of its own continuity from one determinate moment of consciousness to the next. The indifference point between the two functions of thinking is the cancellation of our being and all other being as *agents* of determining activity. This cancellation, Schleiermacher now argues, could not have occurred by means of our own agency of positing. Our activity of positing, as noted above, has itself been canceled. According to Schleiermacher, "This cancellation of contrast, however, could not be *our* consciousness" if therein we were not and would not be a conditioned and determinate consciousness (D429–30). However, we are not conditioned and determined by anything grasped or caught up in contrasts, for example by our own ability to posit.

Schleiermacher concludes that this cancellation of contrasts is not through our own agency. Rather, this break occurs by the agency of the transcendental ground itself (D430). This canceling agency, however, is *not* experienced in terms of a transcendental agency. No positive affirmation is given. Thinking, as we have seen, is in fact negated and can not even be defined except in negative terms.

Accordingly, this canceling agency is to be known simply as the nullification of our own agency. That which cancels our own agency is thus originally known only as *our own* cancellation as agents of our own continuity, as organic agents with the selfsame identity in two distinct but linked moments of consciousness.

A passage found in an 1818 lecture gives further clarification as to how this 'cancellation' of or rising above ourselves as agents of our own determination should be characterized. To understand this passage, we must remember that according to Schleiermacher, we cannot completely describe in thought that which *Anschauung* grasps. This is not surprising. As we have seen, in this state our thinking is not aware of anything. Rather, our thinking is simply the state of its own nullpoint. Thinking is in the state of object-less awareness.

This state cannot be adequately described using either concepts or judgments, because this state involves the cancellation of all concepts and judgments. That which brought about this state of our thinking can initially be described only in negative terms. Concerning this sort of situation, Schleiermacher states that "we could therefore not find what is absolute as concept or judgment. We could conceive it only in negative form, and this is our not-having [*Nichthaben*]" (D153). From the standpoint of objective consciousness, we therefore have nothing to affirm about the agency by means of which thinking is canceled.

Simply stated, we cannot in fact fully encompass [*vollziehen*] "the highest" in thought (D152n). "Why not?" Schleiermacher asks rhetorically in his 1818 lecture. His answer is that "we could only search for it under the form of concept or judgment." If, he continues, we stay with concept, we could not ever remove enough particularity. If we stay with judgment, our combining would not be all-encompassing enough. If, however, we should succeed in stripping off enough particularity from the concept, then it would no longer be a concept; and if we combine our judgment sufficiently, it would no longer be a judgment.

From the standpoint of subjective consciousness, on the other hand, this 'not-having' is caught up in the feeling of life itself. Accordingly, the Supreme Being, in so far as it is actually "in" our self-consciousness, is also the "being of things." This is the case because we, in this moment of immediate self-consciousness, identify our being with all other being that is caught up in the contrast of passivity and activity or spontaneity. This contrast, as we have seen, is canceled. The point of indifference between these two modes of activity is our being (and all other being) canceled as agents of activity. This cancellation of all beings as self-determining agents leads Schleiermacher to characterize the conscious expression of this more original state as "the feeling of universal dependence" (D153 and D430).

Schleiermacher calls the positing of this feeling of dependence in determinate consciousness "the religious element" (D474–75). He also refers to it as "religious feeling" (D430). In this element or feeling, the transcendental ground of determination (or the Supreme Being itself) is represented in human consciousness (D430). Schleiermacher, however, is quite clear that this is a representation, and not the ground itself (D430). Human beings, Schleiermacher is arguing here, do not directly know or experience God.

The Supreme Being is not directly experienced by the self; rather, the Supreme Being is simply represented in consciousness in the form of religious feeling. This representation, however, is unique in that it is not a mediated representation. Rather, it is our immediate feeling of life, along with our felt cancellation as the source of our own determination and the means of our own continuity. Three passages from the *Dialektik* are particularly useful in clarifying this link between the feeling of life and religious feeling.

First, as we learned from the 1831 passage cited above, the cancellation of thinking points to the place where self-consciousness makes itself known to us. We also learned from the 1822 lecture that this cancellation is not through our own agency. Nevertheless, we know this agency only as the cancellation of our own agency as a self-positing being. From the 1818 lecture, we learned that Schleiermacher characterized this conceptualization of any absolute agency of such cancellation as at best our 'not-having' it.

Second, we must realize that Schleiermacher does not characterize this 'not-having' as an actual experience. All experiences are conscious experiences determined by thought and sensations. But thinking and sensations, as we have seen, have been canceled. Why, then, does Schleiermacher even suggest that this 'not-having' could be possible? The answer to this question leads to my third point and takes us into the realm of Schleiermacher's understanding of the transcendental ground of certitude in human experience.

Schleiermacher's investigation of the ground of certitude in thinking led him to investigate the certitude that accompanies the transition from one function to the other. He undertook this quest because this certitude is not based "in" the identity of the two functions (D474). This is so because the point of indifference between the two functions is not the same as the two functions. This certitude is therefore based on that which is beyond these two functions but is nevertheless known as their identity.

Schleiermacher, as we have seen, refers to our immediate state of self-consciousness as the canceling of the thinking self, the not-having of the absolute ground of our own identity, the point of indifference in thinking, and the nullpoint of thought. The 'form' of all conceptualizations regarding this state is that of negation. In keeping with this negative form of expression, Schleiermacher states that the certitude that accompanies the transition from one function to the other is originally co-posited in our self-consciousness as negation (D474–75), as the cessation of both forms of thinking. After that, this certitude is posited in the self-consciousness of people who are thinking in their willing [denkend wollenden] as "dependence on the transcendental ground" (D475).

In other words, certitude does not arise from our own self-possession. In this state, the self is no-thing; there is nothing to possess. Here the self is both object-less and subject-less. This state of self-consciousness is not simply grounded in the identity of both functions but is grounded outside this identity (D475). This certitude, Schleiermacher argues, must therefore be co-posited in self-consciousness originally as that negation: it is *not* the identity of the two functions but their nullpoint. Then, this certainty is posited in the self-activity that belongs to our volitional agency as dependence on a transcendental ground of determination.

The certitude that accompanies immediate self-consciousness is the *certitude of life*. This is the certitude that can never doubt when thinking about this awareness, that the self is alive, a living being, something actual, an organic agent. This certitude has arisen out of the state in which the self does *not* have itself. Schleiermacher can now argue that because the identity of certitude in both functions is precisely the certitude of life, it follows that the transcendental ground from which this certitude arises must also be posited under the form of life (D529). Thus, the source of the self is also posited as life, since life arises from life. Logically this might be the case, but actually we cannot know this. Accordingly, Schleiermacher's argument for a transcendental ground rests on the use of negative description of the self's own sense of continuity as that which is not based on its own agency.

According to Schleiermacher, speculative thinking does not have the need to posit the transcendental ground under the form of life, because philosophic speculation is knowing in and of itself (D529). Speculative thought is removed from the very life pulse that is felt in unmediated self-consciousness. Felt, the relationship is not doubted, for it is already, as it were, 'known'. One is aware of it. Unfelt, it becomes problematical for reason. We can thus understand why the relationship of the transcendental ground to the world is taken to lie at the ground of speculative effort (D529).

The *link* between mind and body, between the intellect and the senses, is the feeling of certitude that arises from our immediate awareness of life itself. This feeling of certitude sanctions our ideas as ultimately referring to, and inextricably linked to, the world in which we live. This certitude of life arises from and is contained in our feeling [*Gefühl*].

The Two Tiers of Feeling

Schleiermacher can refer to the initial stage of the cancellation of the self conceptually in negative terms only. He refers to it as the negation of our two functions. Accordingly, the first tier of feeling can be expressed only in negative form, which is expressed as the cancellation of the agency of the self at the indifference point that makes the transition possible.

This first tier of feeling is precognitive and presensate awareness. This stage of feeling is Schleiermacher's requisite standpoint, comparable to the standpoints that both Beck and Fichte tried to establish as a means of seeing the uncognizable link between thinking and being. Feeling, at this stage, is not a conscious moment. Rather, it is best characterized as the nonreligious, nonphilosophic standpoint at the core of Schleiermacher's work.

The second tier, however, is expressed in an actual, determinate moment of consciousness. This moment of consciousness is the completion of a transition that was accomplished by means of the indifference point. This second tier is a fully determinate moment of consciousness. As we have seen, Schleiermacher refers to this latter moment as the "religious element" (D475) in our actual conscious life.

Schleiermacher represents this second tier, religious consciousness, also at first in negative form only. The second tier is the conscious representation of the more original negative form of this feeling that consciousness can never know. This determinate representation of the transcendental ground is expressed as the feeling of dependence, in contradistinction to the feeling of freedom. Freedom, as we have seen, is the basis of Kant's rational theology.

Schleiermacher has now identified the shift in immediate self-consciousness from the initial preconscious stage of immediate self-consciousness to the subsequent conscious form of immediate self-consciousness. He has done this by distinguishing the two tiers of this experience, with regard to our state of certitude that accompanies the transition from one form of thinking to the other. This shift is initially expressed as the negation of the two functions. Subsequently, this shift is expressed as the feeling of dependence on the transcendental ground of determination. We carry the unity of ourselves as both thinking and being into the unity of the highest power. This unity of ourselves with the highest power is the content of self-consciousness (D517n).

Consciousness of God

Schleiermacher uses the term *God* to express the immediate awareness belonging to the integrity of the I that is carried over from one distinct moment of consciousness to the next. His use of the term also expresses the universal feeling of dependence by the I on a transcendental ground of determination. Consciousness of God is the selfsame transcendental ground (1) for both functions and (2) for the unity of self-consciousness in the transition from one to the other (D525). The first referent pertains to the unity of our thinking; the second pertains to the unity of our organic being. Consciousness of God is the awareness that these two grounds are the same. This conviction of sameness accompanies our individual moments of transition. This conviction is born of the coincidence of *Gefühl* and *Anschauung*.

According to Schleiermacher, the "co-positedness" [*Mitgeseztsein*] of God in our self-consciousness is the essential ground of the unity of our being in the transition from one function of thinking to the other. This co-positedness is represented by religious feeling, the original way in which we are conscious of God (D525n).

The transition between two moments of thinking and concomitantly between two moments of our organic nature are analogous; but the analogy is not complete because our modalities as organic agents are not only those that operate between each moment of thinking but also those that operate *in* each moment of thinking. They are constant and as such accompany all determinate moments of thinking. By maintaining this distinction between feeling and thinking, Schleiermacher is able to maintain his realist principle as that which is beyond the purview of reason. Writes Schleiermacher, *Gefühl* "seems to disappear if we are utterly absorbed in [*aufgeben in*] an *Anschauung* or in an action; but it only appears to disappear" (D429).

On the other hand, this passive (receptive) state of feeling is never present other than as accompanying our determinate states of consciousness. According to Schleiermacher, feeling

> is, however, also always only accompanying. Sometimes it seems to step forth alone and therein to annihilate thought and action; however it only seems so. There are always traces of willing and seeds of thinking or vice versa in both, if also apparently disappearing, in turn, they are co-posited therein (D429).

Schleiermacher argues in an 1818 lecture that if we try to isolate this 'consciousness of God' from our own consciousness of humanity, we will fall into an "unconscious brooding" [*ein bewußtloses Brüten*] (D153). This is so because God-consciousness is experienced "in" our experience of our own immediate self-consciousness that is part of the totality of nature. Schleiermacher explains this connection between our own organic being and the totality of collective organic being most strikingly in an 1822 lecture. The religious human being, Schleiermacher there tells us, is not discontented with this state of affairs, in which we have consciousness of God only "in the fresh and vital consciousness of an earthly consciousness" (D153). Accordingly, we must say that consciousness of God always at all times concerns that which is full of life. Consciousness of God always entails the existence of an other, consciousness of self, distinct human relationships, and the like, and thus the two step forward together (D153).

Thus do we take the unity of our being up with us into the unity of the highest power (D517n), which is co-posited in the initial stage of immediate self-consciousness and subsequently posited as that which accompanies the determinate activity of our own spontaneous agency of thinking.

The fact that our own self-consciousness is expressed in our consciousness of God helps explain why there is a tendency in us to personify the transcendent ground (D532n). This is why Schleier-macher believes that all (positive) religious predications of the term *God* entail anthropomorphism (D475). We "fill in" the content and determine the attributes of God with aspects of our own organic nature that are caught up in our experience of religious feeling.

In Schleiermacher's scheme, the first tier of immediate self-consciousness is the feeling of life. This feeling, however, has its source in the transcendental ground of the self, because the self is not the determining agency of its own continuity: the self's own abil-ity to determine itself has been canceled. This feeling regarding can-cellation is carried over in each transition, just as the actuality of the self is also carried over in each transition to the subsequent determi-nate moment of consciousness (D524). This "carried over" feeling regarding cancellation of the self as a self-determining agency is the second tier of immediate self-consciousness. Schleiermacher refers to this conscious feeling as that of "the transition" [*die Übertragung*]. It refers to that which abides beyond its original negation and is bound to the actuality of life.

This abidingness of the negation of the self as the agency of its own transition is now expressed in (the second tier of) consciousness as the experience of the cancellation of the self's own agency as the source of its life. This conscious awareness of the cancellation of the self as the source of its own agency is expressed as the feeling of dependence on an agency other than the self for self-definition and identity. This "transition" is expressed as the feeling of general dependence—a feeling that is general because the self is identified with all other beings (D474, D430).

In our knowing about knowing, which is the task of dialectic, the transformation of this second tier of the negation of the self in immediate self-consciousness into a positive feeling of actual con-tent is accomplished by means of an accompanying sense of con-viction (D539). The condition for this conviction is "the repose of mind [*Geist*]" (D396), the state of intellection's immediate align-ment with organic being. This repose is based on the certainty that has its ground not in our functions but 'beyond' them as their unity. This unity is felt as life itself. This 'beyond' ourselves of immediate self-consciousness gives repose because we are the sub-ject-less/object-less self awash in life itself.

Hans-Richard Reuter, in his book *Die Einheit der Dialektik Friedrich Schleiermachers*[16], suggests that the feeling of absolute dependence is the "focal point of a plurality of relationships."[17] This plurality of relationships, Reuter argues, does refer to what is absolute. However, within the dialectical critique of metaphysical views, this "Absolute wherein the self sinks is not the *one God*; but the *total world.*"[18] This state, according to Reuter, is "the dialectical . . . reduction of humans to their original humanity.[19] This experience, as Reuter correctly points out, is not necessarily the experience of merging with God. Rather, this experience is the total self at one with the totality of being—the being of the world, of life itself. Here, the self is one with the world, a living sentient drop of being immersed in the living sea of being. This is the embodied self.

Accordingly, the conviction that there is a God does not refer to a determinate fact. Rather, this experience refers to a feeling in which all contrast has been canceled. This cancellation of contrasts, as we have seen, is restful. This is the rest of the contemplative mind, the mind empty of content, the mind in the state of *Anschauung*. This state is simultaneously that of the body awash in the sea of life, indistinguishable from all of life. This is the state of *Gefühl*, the feeling of life itself. This restfulness of body/mind as the coincidence of subject-less/object-less awareness, which abides in the indifference point of thinking and simultaneously the ground of self-continuity beyond self-determination, is the sanctioning ground for transforming our feeling of dependence into an actual affirmation of the transcendental ground as something with its own actual content. According to Schleiermacher, this conviction is the 'place' from which the search for the transcendental begins (D395). "Our knowing about knowing is . . . reflection on the self-consciousness that accompanies it as conviction."[20]

Schleiermacher thereby makes conviction, rather than any actual determinate state of consciousness, the basis for the search for the Absolute. By so doing, he never makes any determinate moment of human consciousness the ultimate ground either for religious conviction or for philosophic certitude.

This feeling of conviction, Schleiermacher claims, is the ground of our conscious search for the transcendental ground of being and thinking. It is the impetus for speculative reason as well as for religious quests. To understand the source of this impetus, we must remember that the core of Schleiermacher's philosophic standpoint pertains to a gap in (objective) self-consciousness. So, too, does the core of his religious standpoint. This core is neither philosophic nor religious, as it is not a determinate moment of consciousness. It is neither thinking [*Denken*] nor sensation [*Empfindung*]. It is not a determinate moment of religious faith, but rather, it is a prereligious, preconceptual state of the self.

Conclusion

The structure of Schleiermacher's overall achievement can be summarized as follows. First, the cancellation of, or rising above thinking is expressed in our organic nature as the rupture, the opening in our own agency as self-positing beings. This break is the place where the pulse of life is felt. Second, this cancellation and this actuality of our life are expressed together by our organic nature, initially (preconsciously) as the cancellation of the self, and subsequently (consciously) as the feeling of negation as a self-determining being by a transcendental ground of determination. Third, this conscious feeling is given the sanction of certitude. This certitude has arisen from the repose of our mental life [*Geist*] in that which is beyond our mental purview, the actuality of life itself. The cancellation of the self as the means of its own continuity is co-posited in us as our transcendental ground of determination, represented in us by a two-tiered feeling of negation. The first tier is not a determinate moment of consciousness; it is simply the feeling of life itself. The second tier of this feeling is the religious element. This tier refers to the religious feeling of dependence on that which is beyond.

The positive predication of religious feeling is the purview of religion, specifically of the doctrine of faith (that is, dogmatics). This predication, however, must follow the canon of all thinking that properly aspires toward knowledge. This canon states (as we shall explore in the final chapter) that 'God' and 'World' are two distinct but inseparable ideas.

The link between philosophy and religion in Schleiermacher's work is the gap itself. This gap is not the religious element. The religious element is expressed as a determinate moment of consciousness, the second tier of immediate self-consciousness. Nor can this gap be a philosophic element because thinking has been canceled. The link between religion and philosophy is the unbounded feeling of life itself aligned with the mind's unmediated openness. Schleiermacher discovered in this unbounded feeling of life, aligned with the mental state of repose the source of our mental and physical certitude that we are alive and are a living unity of experience. Here he also posited the reference for religious feeling as the cancellation of the self's own agency as its own self-determination. This lack of self-determination linked with the feeling of life and coupled with mental repose and a contemplative frame of mind is the conviction that is expressed in a determinate moment of consciousness as religious sentiment. Schleiermacher believed that the philosopher could say nothing more about the term *God* than that it refers to the transcendental ground of thinking avid being. To say anything more is "only bombast or the mixing in of what is religious which, since it does not belong here, must in any case wreak havoc [*verderblich wirken muß*]" (D328).

Schleiermacher maintained a strict distinction between philosophic and religious reflection. The source of this distinction is that which they both have in common and is neither the one nor the other. This common ground of both is human nature as the state of subject-less/object-less awareness that is the fundamental referent for the conviction upon which philosophic and religious thinking reflects. By identifying such a ground, Schleiermacher cleared a space for religious experience that can never be fully expressed by reason (or by religious dogma). This is the legitimate source of his recognition today as the father of modern Protestant theology. He made the referent for religious experience a *human* experience rather than divine revelation, church dogmatics, or the Bible, and, as we have seen, transformed the gap in Kant's theory of the self into the symbolic indication of the hidden ground of our unity.

CHAPTER FIVE

The Embodied Self

From Hegel's standpoint, Schleiermacher's philosophy was the worst of a bad lot. Hegel grouped Schleiermacher with Fichte and Kant (and Friedrich Henrich Jacobi). According to Hegel, these philosophers, in keeping with the tradition of Locke and Hume, attempted to compute and explain the world from the standpoint of the subject.[1] Hegel deemed this to be an unfortunate turn of events. This turn, Hegel argued, is nothing but ordinary human intellect: the culture of reflection, raised to a system.[2] These philosophers begin their philosophic inquiry of the world by investigating the subjective nature of the self.[3] By so doing, Hegel believed that they fell away from the "real ground" and "firm standpoint" of philosophy.[4]

Hegel, like Fichte, believed that intellectual intuition is the "absolute principle of philosophy."[5] Hegel is also in agreement with Fichte that this transcendental principle is at the basis of Kant's deduction of the categories.[6] But unlike both Fichte and Kant, Hegel did not deem the realm of the suprasensuous to be beyond reason's grasp. For Hegel, the true standpoint of philosophy is that of pure knowing, which is the *result* of the progressive determination by consciousness itself from a sheerly subjective state of its own self-awareness as sheer being (a kind of "subjective itch")—a nothing from which something is to proceed, to "the determinate reality *in thought* of what is inner and . . . the *determinateness possessed* by such an inner in this reality."[7]

Philosophy is not concerned with the sheerly inner, Hegel argued, but with the way in which the immediate state of self-consciousness enters into knowing as *thought* "and is enunciated

111

as such."[8] The logic of this process is internally determined, and, accordingly, is self-reliant and independent of accident; it is the necessary function of reason itself (the absolute, the eternal, God), grasping opposites in their unity.

This is Hegel's dialectic; it is speculative thought, self-moving soul, the principle of all natural and spiritual life.[9] Accordingly, dialectic is pure science, knowledge in the entire range of its development with a certainty born of its object internalized and known as itself.[10] Such a logic, for Hegel, "is the only true standpoint."[11] It is liberation from the opposition of consciousness, because as the object of its own thought its object is equally pure thought. Accordingly, truth, as science, is pure self-consciousness in its self-development and has the shape of itself. Objective thinking is the content of pure science, and logic is the realm of pure thought thinking itself, that is, the system of pure reason. Unmediated, this realm is "without veil" because it is in its own absolute nature.

The content of logic, accordingly, is the delineation of the self-movement of the absolute, "the exposition of God as he is in his eternal essence before the ratio of nature and a finite mind."[12] From such a perspective, logic is not discourse *about* God, but God's discourse, God's thought—the discourse *of* God.[13] Hegel believed that Kant and Fichte mistakenly staked their philosophic claims to the "fixed standpoint" of reason affected by sensibility, and that by so doing, Fichte and Kant set their sights on the science of human cognition rather than on the cognition of God.[14]

Alexandre Kojève, in his *Introduction to the Reading of Hegel: Lectures on the Phenomenology of Spirit*, characterized this Hegelian standpoint as theology, "that is, the logic, thought or discourse of God"[15] because Hegel's logic became God's (or vice versa!). To avoid such hubris, Kojève suggests that we must claim that "the natural World eludes *conceptual* understanding" and recognize Hegel's logic as a dialectic for "Man and History."[16]

More than a century before Kojève, Schleiermacher, in his own 'correction' of the Hegelian system, explained why the natural world eludes reason. Believing that Hegel's system, among others, did not escape the one-sided reliance on reason that plagued the philosophies of both Kant and Fichte, Schleiermacher argued that *feeling [Gefühl]* is the completion of that which no transcendental formula for God can grasp. Such formulae for God as Absolute Subject, First Cause, Providence, Fate, Lawgiver, Creator are expressions of the intellectual function in thinking. No state of thinking (even that of *Anschauung*) could glimpse the transcendental ground (D430–31). Feeling cannot be simply absorbed by reason because feeling is reason's nullpoint, the unity of contrasts that cannot be thought because it is the cancellation of thought. Schleiermacher also believed that feeling [*Gefühl*] becomes the representation of the transcendental ground in our determinate self-consciousness. This representation, he argued, is "the completion of the erring and deficient unity" provided by all formulae that rely sheerly on the activity of thinking.

According to Schleiermacher, feeling can never be taken up into speculative thought, because feeling is in us as the identity of contrasts (D431). This contrast between the intellectual and organic functions in thinking, as we have seen, entails a feeling that is expressed in thinking only as certitude regarding life itself and in the belief that we are dependent on a transcendental ground for our determination. This feeling is originally expressed in objective consciousness only as the nullpoint of thinking and the 'not-having' of the Absolute. Feeling is the identity of the two functions of thinking. This feeling, however, is never merely something past, because this identity is life itself. This feeling is the subjective reality of the unbounded self at one with the world. This feeling of life is in and between every moment of objective consciousness but it cannot be thought. This feeling of life is also the place of the negation of our organic nature as the source of its own agency.

The unity with the world which this feeling brings to the fore with the nullpoint of thinking cannot be replaced by thinking. Speculative thought is not, and cannot replace, the feeling of unity ushered in by unmediated or immediate self-consciousness (D431). It cannot do so because this feeling is that of life itself. Thinking at this point is null. Accordingly, thinking is not, and can never cognize, this feeling.

Reflection that is focused on feeling and is not grasped in scientific endeavors can bring forth transcendental formulae only in a subordinate sense (D431). These formulae are abstractions. Speculative activity, on the other hand, is directed toward the elucidation of these abstractions. Accordingly, reflection cannot do without speculative activity. The involvement of speculative activity in religious reflection is among other things the source of all anthropomorphism in the natural theology of the philosophers.

To mitigate against this anthropomorphic tendency, all reflection about religious feeling should stay within the language of formulae that entail the contrasts of the organic and intellectual functions in thinking. Twofoldness [*Duplicität*] must thereby be the rule for all such formulae. This, as we saw in chapter three, is Schleiermacher's master key to reason that wills to know [*Wollenwissen*]. The place for such reflection, however, is not in philosophy but in dogmatics (that is, *Glaubenslehre*, Doctrine of Faith) (D431). Schleiermacher's description of Kant's moral philosophy as a "veiled dogmatic" thus pertains to Kant's use of speculative reason to develop formulae for the transcendental ground as philosophic concerns.

The Two Canons of Schleiermacher's *Dialektik*

As we saw in chapter four, Schleiermacher believes that the transcendental presupposition of all (objective) thinking is that thinking must correspond to being and vice versa (D518). This presupposition is transcendental, because being is never directly perceived or thought; rather, being is always mediated by organic affections and by the activity of reason. In other words, we are aware of being only by means of our determinate thinking—by means of concepts and judgments about being (D404). Concepts are the form being is given in consciousness and judgments in their totality constitute the totality of being. The two, when complete, are identical (D519).

Schleiermacher can now define the totality of being as our idea of the world. This idea, Schleiermacher argues, is a transcendental presupposition because the world is never directly perceived by thinking; it is only thought about (D432–33). Accordingly, to discuss the world is to discuss our *idea* of the world as a plurality of being. All such discussions presuppose a unity of being.

The term *God* refers to the *idea* of the unity of being that is presupposed by the idea of the world (as the plurality of being). Concerning this, Schleiermacher states in an 1822 lecture, "Indeed, logically one can think the relationship **God = unity with the exclusion of all contrasts; world = unity with the inclusion of all contrasts**" (D433). Schleiermacher suggests that a real (as opposed to a merely logical) expression of the relationship between the world and that through which it emerges into expression can be stated as follows: There must be in being something (x) that the being of the world as a plurality presupposes and through which it has emerged. Further, there must be a logical expression that corresponds to this x.

The previous citation, Schleiermacher argues, is the logical expression of this correspondence (D433).

Accordingly, the terms *God* and *World* represent the two components of Schleiermacher's transcendental formula for all objective thinking. *God*, as the unity of being, is that to which concepts ultimately refer in thinking. *World*, as the totality of being, is that to which all judgments ultimately refer in thinking. As we have seen, concepts and judgments are the two modes by means of which all objective thinking occurs. Accordingly, the transcendental presupposition of the unity of these two distinct modes is expressed as the transcendental presupposition of the unity of the two distinct ideas *God* and *World*.

These two terms refer to two fundamental ideas, neither of which can be given adequate expression without including the perspective of the other. If, for instance, the absolute unity of being is expressed, then this presupposes the nullification of the plurality of being and vice versa. An adequate expression of one term necessitates the inclusion of the expression of the other term as its accompanying presupposition. In other words, the unity of being (God) presupposes that this unity exists in relation to the plurality of being (World) and vice versa. The two ideas to which these two terms refer are thus correlative (D162).

According to Schleiermacher, all adequate formulae for the transcendental ground must entail the two ideas: 'God' and 'World'. One expression without the other is inadequate for the purpose. Each idea, however, is distinct and cannot be reduced to the other. These two formulae constitute the basic canons of Schleiermacher's *Dialektik*. The first canon is: The world cannot be thought about without thinking about God (D167, D432). The second canon is: The two ideas are not the same (D168). According to Schleiermacher, these two canons are totally adequate as grounds for his dialectical task (D168).

These two ideas (God and World) are not identical. Each refers to a differently conceived determining ground of consciousness. These two ideas, however, cannot be totally separated from each other because they "are only two values for the self-same claim" (D433–34). That is, in this context, and only in this context, the two terms (*God* and *World*) express the limits of our discourse about the transcendental ground of thinking and being. These limits are known as the actuality of life itself (the 'World') and the agency, as the unity of being for cancellation of the purely self-determining activity of the self ('God').

The question necessarily arises as to how these two constitutive values of thinking relate to each other (D431–32; D434). According to Schleiermacher, we cannot answer this question in positive terms because both *God* and *World* in this context are transcendental terms. They demarcate the limit and the presupposition of all actual thinking. We can know neither as other than through our thinking and our ideas; and each of the two ideas can be determined only as each is co-related to the other. Each, as we have seen, is the terminus of the other. The two meet at their common border. This border, as we have seen, is feeling. Feeling is not comprised by either idea but refers to their unity. This unity is self-consciousness; the unmediated awareness of life itself, the state of subject-less [*Gefühl*] and object-less [*Anschauung*] awareness. *Gefühl* is the "stimulus" of *Anschauung*; it is the source of the mind's overarching attitude of life-affirming certitude.

For Schleiermacher, philosophy, at its most basic level of orientation or direction, should be understood as a knowing of life or the world. It is thinking directed toward the world (D435). Philosophy thinks *about* feeling; it cannot think feeling. Cognitive thinking and organic being are codeterminate and aligned but they are not the same thing. This is the heart of Schleiermacher's canon.

Schleiermacher uses the language of medieval theology to express the co-terminus relationship between the two ideas God and World. These two ideas relate to each other as *terminus a quo* (God) and *terminus ad quem* (World) and describe the direction in which a person is moving in one's knowing (D434). Both directions, however, are directions of 'thinking on the way to knowing' (D433). Both directions must remain within the rules and principles of the canon of all adequate thinking. Nevertheless, Schleiermacher claims that the 'idea of the deity' [*Idee der Gottheit*] refers to both the limit from which and to which all thinking refers. It relates itself to our thinking equally as *terminus a quo* and *ad quem*. Schleiermacher arrives at this conclusion in the following way.

The World, according to Schleiermacher, refers not simply to nature but to the in-one-another of nature and mind [*Geist*] (D526n). This union is that which Schleiermacher means by the term *Denken*. Accordingly, the efficacy of *Geist* is co-posited in being. This co-relatedness is expressed in the literal designation of 'philosophy' in German as 'world-wisdom' [*Weltweisheit*]. This relationship is grasped as reciprocally both physical knowing, about the physical aspect of nature including the human body, and ethical knowing, about the human aspect of the world.

The idea of the world is only the limit of thinking. This limit is that from which our thinking emerges. The 'World' simply demarcates the limit of our concepts and judgments; it is never without reference to our manifold of sense impressions. Accordingly, Schleiermacher asserts that the World can be expressed only as the *terminus ad quem* and not as the *terminus a quo* (D434).

On the other hand, the ground of our thinking that is still more transcendental than that regarding the 'World' is to be expressed by us always and only as that which we posit as 'God' (D526). This more transcendental ground is not merely the limit of our world but also that which is outside [*außerhalb*] the world (D526n). This difference between the two transcendental grounds of thinking is represented by the second component of Schleiermacher's canon. This element denies that the two ideas are identical. God is also the ground of the World. God is the ground of both nature and *Geist*. These two together, as we have seen, constitute the 'World' (D526n).

Schleiermacher knew that only a model that held both identity and difference to be co-determinate factors in thinking could solve the problem of the gap in Kant's critical philosophy. Schleiermacher solved the problem of the gap by recognizing *the feeling that exceeds the reach of reason* and is *the sanctioning ground of certitude* for both faith and knowing. This feeling is that which arises at the point where nature and mind meet. Thinking, here, is in repose.

As was noted in chapter four, Schleiermacher believes that only religious interests motivate a fuller treatment of the relation of these two ideas. Such interests are justified, but they always contain anthropomorphic elements, because the "religious element" always entails self-awareness. The task of the *Dialektik* is to examine such thinking and conform it to the principles discovered by the *Dialektik*. Only when the thinking entailed in these religious interests is conformed to the principles established as the ground of all correct thinking can thinking in the religious domain be deemed knowing (D168). Schleiermacher is thus able to sidestep Hegel's logic and keep religious *thinking* within the rules of 'correct thinking' without reducing discourse about God to 'God's own discourse'. For Schleiermacher, positive, determinate cognition of the transcendental ground is always mediated by ideas. The "religious element" itself has its source in thinking's nullpoint and as such cannot be cognized; it is not a concept. The concept of *Gefühl*, as we have seen, allowed Schleiermacher to move beyond the "appearance of atheism" of Kant's rational theology as well as the arrogance of Hegel's speculative system, and instead affirm life's sacred integrity without making reason the sanctioning ground of this experience. Schleiermacher's success has bequeathed to us a legacy that allows us securely to affirm the integrity and coherence of our lives without necessitating the same sure affirmation of our specific ideas about life. All such ideas, as we have seen, are incomplete. Accordingly, all religious claims are also incomplete.

Conclusion

Schleiermacher anointed the gap that Kant left and Hegel tried to bridge. In this regard, Richard Crouter's assessment of Hegel's attempt to bridge the "breach" in Kant's critical philosophy is worth citing at length. Crouter, in his essay "Hegel and Schleiermacher at Berlin: A Many-Sided Debate," writes that

> As best I can make out, Hegel sees Schleiermacher as being too uncritically a Kantian (broadly defined). In his [Hegel's] view, Schleiermacher accepts the reduction of knowledge to the realm of finite objects, but then seeks to get beyond this reduction at the level of intuition and feeling. For his part Hegel attempts to get beyond Kant through a more thoroughgoing effort at describing and identifying all the antinomies of thought. Hegel's philosophy of spirit is an attempt to heal the breach between the external world, self-consciousness, and our consciousness of the world. . . .[17]

From Hegel's perspective, Schleiermacher excluded reason from the deepest and holiest contents of our experience.[18] This is exactly what Schleiermacher strove to do, in a quite thoroughgoing way. Schleiermacher tried to show that reason can never grasp this birthplace of religion, because reason, at this moment, reaches its nullpoint. As he said in *On Religion*, our body lies in the bosom of the infinite world and every sinew and muscle of our body feels infinite life as its own. Here we discover life—all of it, because we are life; we embody it and it embodies us.

Notes

Introduction

1. Postmodern a/theologian Mark C. Taylor, in recounting "the epoch of selfhood" from Augustine's *Confessions* to Hegel's *Phenomenology of Spirit*, states "that it is not too much to suggest that Western philosophy and theology reached closure in the Hegelian system." (*Erring: A Postmodern A/theology*, Chicago: The University of Chicago Press, 1984, pp. 14, 83, and 98.)

Ronald M. Green, in his book *Kierkegaard and Kant: The Hidden Debt* (Albany: State University of New York Press, 1992, pp. 49–50), suggests that Kierkegaard rather than Schleiermacher should be viewed as the end of another line of post-Kantian thinkers including Ritschl and Hermann who "ultimately" benefitted from the "explosion" and impact of the deeply religious side of Kant's critical philosophy. Green convincingly argues that "A major and overarching similarity between Kierkegaard and Kant has to do with their shared conviction that 'the ethical is the universal' (95)" and that "'willing the Good' is the sole thing that unites human beings (99)." As we shall see, Schleiermacher believed that such perspectives were "one-sided." He strove to correct this imbalance in his *Dialektik* by redefining the ethical subject. By so doing, he made it possible to understand more clearly the meaning of his claims in *Christian Faith* (English Translation of the Second German Edition, eds. H. R. Mackintosh and J. S. Stewart, Philadelphia: Fortress Press, 1976) that (1) a distinctness of feeling [*eine Bestimmtheit des Gefühls*] is the basis of all ecclesiastical communions (paragraph 3), and that (2) such piety is passed on from one generation to the next, is as old as the self-propagating human race and accordingly, is a universal element of human life (paragraph 61, 4).

2. Wolfgang Carl, "Kant's First Drafts of the Deduction of the Categories," *Kant's Transcendental Deductions*, ed. Eckart Förster (Stanford: Stanford University Press, 1989), pp. 5 and 18.

3. Eckart Förster, "Kant's Selbstsetzungslehre," *Kant's Transcendental Deductions*, pp. 229–35. I am especially indebted to the work of this Kantian scholar in identifying the precise ways in which the gap in Kant's critical theory evolved.

4. Alexandre Kojève summarizes this evaluation of Kant's doctrine of the self in his book *Introduction to the Reading of Hegel: Lectures on the Phenomenology of Spirit*, trans. J. H. Nicholas (Ithaca: Cornell University Press, 1969), p. 130. "Man, as historical being, remains inexplicable: neither the World of *concrete* things in which he lives, nor the History that he creates by *temporal* free acts, is understood."

5. Dieter Henrich, *Fichtes ursprüngliche Einsicht* (Frankfurt: Klostermann, 1967), p. 16. English translation by David R. Lachterman, "Fichte's Original Insight," *Contemporary German Philosophy* I (University Park: Pennsylvania State University Press, 1982), p. 23. I am in agreement with Manfred Frank (*Das individuelle Allgemeine: Textstrukturierung und -interpretation nach Schleiermacher* [Frankfurt a.M.: Suhrkamp, 1985] p. 94ff.) that Henrich's essay and the new Fichte scholarship it has inspired have been remiss in not taking into account Schleiermacher's own penetrating insights into the inadequacies of a reflection model for a viable theory of self-consciousness.

6. Hegel, *The Difference Between Fichte's and Schelling's System of Philosophy*, trans. H. S. Harris and Walter Cerf. Albany: State University of New York Press, 1977, p. 173.

7. Ibid., p. 170.

8. Richard Crouter, "Hegel and Schleiermacher at Berlin: A Many-Sided Debate" (*Journal of the American Academy of Religion*, Vol. 48, 1980), pp. 33–41.

9. Crouter cites Adolph von Harnack on this same issue (p. 34). Writes Harnack: "Schleiermacher feared the despotism of Hegelian philosophy and at least the Academy was to be kept free of it" (*Geschichte der königlich preußichen Akademie der Wissenschaften zu Berlin*, 1/2, Berlin: Reichsdruckerei), p. 735.

10. Gordon E. Michalson, Jr., in his book *Fallen freedom: Kant on radical evil and moral regeneration* (Cambridge: Cambridge University Press, 1990), pp. 78–79, suggests that a recognition of the "rigid dual-

ism" born of "the absence of any principle of integration between the noumenal-moral and the phenomenal-temporal" helps elucidate the impossibility of explaining how we can speak of the moral disposition of the Kantian ethical subject in temporal terms.

11. Rudolf Odebrecht, "Das Gefüge des religiosen Bewußtseins bei Fr. Schleiermacher," (*Blätter für Deutsche Philosophie*, 1934–35, Vol. 8), p. 287. Odebrecht demonstrates that Eberhard sought the place between actual knowledge and the mere desire for it and granted to feeling [*Gefühl*] this place of transition, the bridge from one area to the other by means of which the great gap could be filled. For Eberhard, this gap separated the supranatural from appearance. Odebrecht suggests that here might lie the "very first seeds and stimulations," the development of which had been assisted by Kant's three *Critiques*. Odebrecht believes that Schleiermacher apparently adopted but altered Eberhard's structure.

12. Emanuel Hirsch, *Geschichte der Neuern Evangelischen Theologie*, vol. 5 (Gütersloh: C. Bertelsmann Verlag, 1949).

13. Ibid., pp. 298–99. As Rudolf Odebrecht has suggested in his essay "Das Gefüge des religiösen Bewußtseins bei Fr. Schleiermacher," p. 285, Schleiermacher's unheard of power of conceptual analysis extracted the logical-ontological basis of existence from the traditional representations of God as *natura naturans*, creator or ruler, fate, and providence and over against this tradition emphasized the "ungivenness" [*Ungegebenheit*] of the transcendent ground.

Martin Heidegger's investigation of "the god-less thinking" [*das gott-lose Denken*] that must relinquish the "God of philosophy, God as *causa sui*," in order to "perhaps be nearer to the divine God" is strikingly resonant with Schleiermacher's own attempt more than a century earlier to move beyond the confines of "modern" Western metaphysics' conflation of the *idea of God* with *that to which the idea refers* (D436). ("Die Onto-Theo-Logische Verfassung der Metaphysik," *Identität und Differenz*, Pfullingen: Günther Neske, 1957, p. 71; English translation, "The Onto-theo-logical Nature of Metaphysics," *Essays in Metaphysics: Identity and Difference*, trans. Kurt F. Leidecker, New York: Philosophical Library, Inc., p. 65). Heidegger referred to this Western conflation of expression and ground as an onto-theo-logic affirmation of *God* as the cause of being and *thought* as the expression of being (g. p. 56ff; e. p. 52ff).

In this regard, Robert P. Scharlemann correctly affirms in *Theology at the End of the Century* (Charlottesville: University Press of Virginia, 1990, p. 6), that "Heidegger's own account of theology in his essay *Phänomenologie und Theologie* of 1928 is not unlike the account given by Schleiermacher at the beginning of his dogmatics, *Christian Faith*. Even Schleiermacher's use of the term 'the whence,' rather than 'the cause', to designate the intentionality in religious feeling . . . indicates a break with this kind of ontotheology," (p. 118).

14. Hirsch, pp. 298–99.

15. Hans-Richard Reuter, *Die Einheit der Dialektik Friedrich Schleiermachers: Eine systematische Interpretation* (München: Chr. Kiser Verlag, 1979).

16. Reuter, p. 17.

17. Paul Frederick Mehl, *Schleiermacher's Mature Doctrine of God as Found in the Dialektik of 1822 and the Second Edition of The Christian Faith (1830–31)*, dissertation, Columbia University, 1961.

18. Mehl, p. 283. Citing Schleiermacher's own characterization of his Introduction to *Christian Faith* in *Schleiermachers Sendschreiben über seine Glaubenslehre an Lücke*, p. 21.

19. Mehl's sensitive treatment of the precognitive feeling that preceeds religious consciousness was important in focusing my own attention on this distinction within Schleiermacher's treatment of religious consciousness.

20. In the second appendix to his dissertation, Mehl uses the insights of Emanuel Hirsch, "one of the few scholars writing on Schleiermacher to have made use of Odebrecht's edition of the *Dialektik*," to provide the reader with a philosophic and theological context for Schleiermacher's doctrine of God (p. 295).

21. Mehl, p. ii.

22. See John E. Thiel's book *God and World in Schleiermacher's Dialektik and Glaubenslehre* (Bern: Peter Lang, 1981), p. 10.

23. Richard B. Brandt, *The Philosophy of Schleiermacher: The Development of His Theory of Scientific and Religious Knowledge* (New York: Harper & Row Publishers, 1941).

24. Gerhard Spiegler, *Schleiermacher's Experiment in Cultural Theology: The Eternal Covenant* (New York: Harper & Row Publishers, 1967).

25. John E. Thiel's latest book, *Imagination and Authority: Theological Authorship in the Modern Tradition* (Minneapolis: Fortress Press, 1991), in its delineation and discussion of theological authorship as one of the characteristics definitive of post-Enlightenment theology (p. 8), is a important text. Thiel, however, by keeping his discussion of Christian theology centered in "the authoritative givenness of divine revelation as the basis of its reflection," (p. 197) cannot adequately take into account the way in which

Schleiermacher stepped outside this tradition in his *Dialektik* by making the most elemental stage of religious self-consciousness an a-religious stage that cannot make positive claims about divine revelation.

26. Charles Hartshorne proffers an apt definition of *panentheism* in his book *The Divine Relativity: A Social Conception of God* (New Haven: Yale University Press, 1948), p. 89: "If 'pantheism' is a historically and etymologically appropriate term for the view that deity is the all of relative or independent items, with nothing wholly independent or in any clear sense nonrelative, then 'panentheism' is an appropriate term for the view that deity is in some real aspect distinguishable from and independent of any and all relative items and yet, taken as an actual whole, includes all relative items." From this standpoint, God is both absolutely relative and absolute; changing and changeless.

27. Carl, "Kant's First Drafts," pp. 18–19.

28. Herman-J. de Vleeschauwer, *La Déduction Transcendentale dans L'Oeuvre de Kant* (Paris: Librairie Ernest Leroux, 1934–1937).

29. Herman-J. de Vleeschauwer, *The Development of Kantian Thought: The History of a Doctrine*, trans. A. R. C. Duncan (Toronto: Thomas Nelson and Sons Ltd., 1962), pp. 1–2. Originally published as *L'Évolution de la pensée Kantienne*, Presses Universitaires du France, 1939.

30. Friedrich Schleiermacher, *On the Glaubenslehre: Two Letters to Dr. Lücke*, trans. James Duke and Francis Fiorenza (Chico: Scholars Press, 1981), p. 57. Writes Schleiermacher: "I presumed—and I did not fail to say so—that all would somehow bring along with them in their immediate self-consciousness what was missing, so that no one would feel short-changed, even though the content was not presented in dogmatic form until later."

31. In *Christian Faith*, Schleiermacher suggests that "It is clear, to begin with, that the antithesis between the inability to inform all moments of life with the feeling of absolute dependence and the corresponding ability communicated to us by the Redeemer, presupposes that feeling itself and a knowledge of it. . . . It might, however, be said that such facts of the religious self-consciousness, which precede fellowship with the Redeemer, cannot belong to the system of *Christian* doctrine, but only to some general system of doctrine, or to the system of some religious communion from which one should pass to Christianity. To this we must reply that these states of the religious mind do not disappear when the mind has been laid hold

of by Christianity, but are facilitated and encouraged in proportion as the communicated capacity is less or more" (paragraph 29, 1).

32. *Lücke*, p. 37.

33. *Lücke*, pp. 34–35.

34. *Lücke*, p. 36.

35. *Schleiermachers Sendschreiben über seine Glaubenslehre an Lücke*, von Lic. Hermann Mulert, 10. We should not lose sight of the irony imbedded in Schleiermacher's "best defense." What was self-evident for Schleiermacher remained undisclosed to his critics. Schleiermacher, by claiming the evidence of his own awareness of who he really is, committed anew his original offense. Schleiermacher's self-evidence of identity remained non-evidence for his critics.

36. Ulrich Barth, *Christentum und Selbstbewußtsein* (Göttingen: Vandenhöck & Ruprecht, 1983), pp. 7–27.

37. Friedrich Schleiermacher, *Schleiermacher's Introduction to Plato's Dialogues*, trans. William Dobson (New York: Arno Press, 1973), pp. 16–17.

38. Ibid., pp. 17–18.

39. Ibid., p. 47. The impact of Plato on Schleiermacher's struggle with Kant's critical philosophy is beyond the scope of this present work and will not be pursued.

40. Ibid., p. 17.

41. Ibid., p. 17.

42. Ibid., p. 7.

43. Odebrecht's discussion of the primary and secondary stages of religious consciousness in his essay "Das Gefüge des religiösen Bewußtseins bei Fr. Schleiermacher" is remarkably insightful and played a crucial role in helping me identify the pre-conscious stage of religious experience. Nevertheless, I find Odebrecht's analysis limited by two factors. First, although Odebrecht affirms that the feeling of absolute dependence is not the core of religious consciousness (p. 296), he nevertheless describes the original stage of this experience as a "fullness of transcendence" [*Erfülltsein von Transzendenz*] (p. 292). This fullness, however, is not a direct referent to the self's experience of God as the transcendent ground of thinking and being. Schleiermacher denied the possibility of positive predication of the transcendent ground at this primordial stage of self-consciousness. (D153; D474–75). Here, I am in agreement with Paul Frederick Mehl, who also takes issue with Odebrecht's incautious statement (*Schleiermacher's Mature Doctrine of God as*

Found in the Dialektik of 1822 and the Second Edition of The Christian Faith (1830–31) p. 105). Second, Odebrecht does not take Schleiermacher's 1831 lectures into account in this discussion. This greatly reduces the explanatory power of his essay because these lectures clarify the subsequent stage of religious consciousness that transforms the preconscious stage of self-consciousness into a fully predicated, positive description of the content of religious experience.

44. Schleiermacher wrote this statement in his July 19, 1800, letter to his lifelong friend Gustav von Brinkman (*Aus Schleiermachers Leben in Briefen*, vol. 4, p. 73). This citation is taken from Albert L. Blackwell's book, *Schleiermacher's Early Philosophy of Life: Determinism, Freedom and Phantasy*, (Chico, California: Scholars Press, 1982), p. 163.

45. Martin Redeker, *Schleiermacher: Life and Thought*, trans. John Wallhausser (Philadelphia: Fortress Press, 1973), pp. 40ff.

46. Redeker, 40.

47. Lücke, p. 19.

48. Redeker, p. 41.

Chapter 1. Kant's Problem

1. Cited by Richard Crouter in his introduction to his translation of Schleiermacher's book *On Religion: Speeches to Its Cultured Despisers* (Cambridge: Cambridge University Press, 1988), p. 19.

2. Martin Redeker, *Schleiermacher's Life and Thought*, trans. John Wallhausser (Philadelphia: Fortress Press, 1973), pp. 12ff.

3. Letter to his father (August 14, 1787) in *The Life of Schleiermacher as Unfolded in His Autobiography and Letters*, Vol. I, trans. Frederica Rowan (London: Smith, Elder & Co., 1860), p. 68.

4. Ibid.

5. Redeker, pp. 7ff.

6. Ibid., p. 9.

7. Ibid., p. 9. See *Briefe Schleiermachers*, Band I, ed. Hermann Mulert (Berlin: Im Propyläen-Verlag, 1923), pp. 294–95.

8. Redeker, p. 9.

9. Ibid., pp. 9–11.

10. Ibid., p. 13.

11. Ibid, p. 14; in Albert L. Blackwell's book *Schleiermacher's Early Philosophy of Life: Determinism, Freedom and Phantasy* (Chico, California: Scholars Press, 1982), p. 7.

12. Cited by Blackwell in *Schleiermacher's Early Philosophy of Life*, 7–8. Schleiermacher's letter to his father, Jan. 21, 1887. *Briefe* I, pp. 42–43.

13. Ibid., p. 8. Feb. 8, 1787. *Briefe*, I, p. 46 and p. 49.

14. Letter from his father (May 17, 1787). Rowan, pp. 65–66.

15. Redeker, p. 15.

16. Crouter, p. 19.

17. Ibid., p. 19.

18. Redeker, p. 15.

19. Letter to Brinkmann (February 2, 1790). Cited by Crouter in his introduction to *On Religion*, pp. 19–20. See *Friedrich Schleiermacher Kritische Gesamtausgabe Schriften und Entwürfe*, [KGA], Band V.1, eds. Andreas Arndt and Wolfgang Virmond (Berlin, 1985) p. 191, no. 134.

20. Redeker, p. 16. Not only were Schleiermacher's father and uncle Reformed ministers, that is, ministers of the Calvinistic rather than the Lutheran Church, but so also were Schleiermacher's paternal grandfather and his maternal grandfather and great grandfather.

21. Friedrich Schleiermacher, "Über das höchste Gut," *Friedrich Schleiermacher Kritische Gesamtausgabe Schriften und Entwürfe* [KGA], Band I. 1, ed. Günter Meckenstock (Berlin: Walter de Gruyter, 1984) pp. 81–125. English translation: *On the Highest Good*, trans. H. Victor Froese, *Schleiermacher: Studies-and-Translations* vol. 10 (Lewistown, New York: The Edwin Mellen Press, 1992).

22. Blackwell's book *Schleiermacher's Early Philosophy of Life* is a first-rate study of these earliest philosophic tracts by Schleiermacher.

23. KGA I, pp. 100–101.

24. Friedrich Schleiermacher, *Grundlinien einer Kritik der bisherigen Sittenlehre*, *Friedrich Schleiermacher's Sämmtliche Werke*, III, 1. Berlin: Georg Reimer, 1846.

25. Blackwell, p. 22.

26. Emil L. Fackenheim, "Immanuel Kant," *Nineteenth Century Religious Thought in the West*, vol. 1, eds. Ninian Smart, John Clayton, Patrick Sherry, and Steven T. Katz (Cambridge: Cambridge University Press, 1985).

27. Ibid., p. 29.

28. Ibid., pp. 29–30.

29. Ibid., p. 28.

30. Ibid., p. 23.

31. Ibid.

32. Odebrecht, "Das Gefüge," p. 301.

33. Ibid., p. 298.

34. Blackwell, p. 88. See Wilhelm Dilthey's *Leben Schleiermachers*, 1st ed., the appendix entitled "Denkmale," p. 140.

35. Friedrich Schleiermacher, *Über die Religion: Reden an die Gebildeten unter ihren Verächtern* (Hamburg: Felix Meiner, 1958).

36. Ibid., pp. 41–42. Crouter, pp. 112-13.

37. This citation is from a translation of Friedrich Schleiermacher's *Über die Religion: Reden an die gebildeten unter ihren Verächtern*, Dritte Auflage (Berlin, 1821), with reference to the critical edition of all the original editions by G. Ch. Bernhard Pünjer (Braunschweig, 1879), by Terrence N. Tice. *On Religion: Addresses in Response to its Cultured Critics* (Richmond, Virginia: John Knox Press, 1969), p. 87.

38. Michalson, *Fallen freedom*, p. 69.

39. Eckart Förster, "Is there a 'Gap' in Kant's Critical System?," *Journal of the History of Philosophy* 25:4 (October, 1987), p. 551. Vleeschauwer, pp. 179ff.

40. Herman-J. de Vleeschauwer, *The Development of Kantian Thought: The History of a Doctrine*, translated by A. R. C. Duncan. Thomas Nelson and Sons Ltd., London, 1962, p. 79. Originally published as *L'Évolution de la pensée Kantienne*, Presses Universitaires de France, 1939.

41. Förster, "Is there a 'Gap,'" pp. 540–550.

42. Ibid., p. 541.

43. Ibid., pp. 540–41.

44. Ibid., p. 541.

45. Ibid., p. 550.

46. Eckart Förster, "Kant's *Selbstsetzungslehre*," *Kant's Transcendental Deductions*, ed. Eckart Förster (Stanford: Stanford University Press, 1989), p. 229.

47. Förster, "Is there a 'Gap,'" p. 548.

48. Ibid., p. 523. See Kant to J. G. C. C. Kiesewetter, Oct. 19, 1798 (Zweig, 252).

49. As Förster affirms, "Kant wavers—for at least a while—in his assessment of the status of the ether" as to whether it exists outside the idea of it, in the idea of it, or merely as a thought object ("Is there a 'Gap,'" p. 226).

50. Förster, "Kant's *Selbstsetzungslehre*," p. 226.

51. Burkhard Tuschling, "Apperception and Ether: On the Idea of a Transcendental Deduction of Matter in Kant's *Opus postumum*," *Kant's Transcendental Deductions*, ed. Eckart Förster.

52. Ibid., p. 212.

53. Ibid., p. 213.

54. Ibid., p. 216.

55. Förster, "Kant's *Selbstsetzungslehre*," p. 226.

56. Jules Vuillemin, "Kant's Dynamics," *Kant's Transcendental Deductions.*

57. Ibid., p. 247.

58. Vleeschauwer, *The Development of Kantian Thought*, pp. 96–97.

59. Dilthey, *Leben Schleiermachers*, vol. 2, ed. Martin Redeker, *Wilhelm Dilthey's Gesammelte Schriften*, vol. 14 (Göttingen: Vandenhöck & Ruprecht, 1966), p. 71.

60. Rowan, I, p. 68.

61. Michalson, *Fallen freedom*, p. 8.

62. As Wolfgang Carl notes in his essay, "Kant's First Drafts of the Deduction," p. 20, Kant in his *Reflexionen* defines the notion of apperception as designating "the relation of all representations to their common subject." The subject relates all of its representations to itself as "a thinking subject in general." This manner of relating all of its representations to itself generates the representation 'I think' in the subject. This designation represents the subject's "perception" of itself as thinking. Apperception is this relation by the subject of all representations to itself as one self-identical unity, that is, the self's general consciousness of itself as a thinking subject.

63. Henrich, "Kant's Notion of a Deduction," *Kant's Transcendental Deductions*, pp. 42–46.

64. Ibid., p. 42.

65. Ibid., p. 46.

66. Ibid.

67. Ibid.

68. Ibid.

69. Henrich, "Fichte's Original Insight," p. 23.

70. Ibid., pp. 18–19, p. 23.

71. Herman-J. de Vleeschauwer, *La Déduction Transcendentale dans L'Oeuvre de Kant*, vols. I–III, Paris: Librairie Ernest Leroux, 1934–1937.

72. Vleeschauwer, *The Development of Kantian Thought: The History of a Doctrine*, p. 45.

73. Vleeschauwer, *La Déduction*, III, p. 291.

74. Ibid.

75. Vleeschauwer, *La Déduction*, II, p. 412.

76. Schleiermacher, *Drittes Tagebuch, Leben Schleiermachers*, Dilthey, "Denkmale," p. 147. Also of KGA III.1 (1988), ed. Gunter Meckenstock, "Gedanken," p. 320.

77. Johann Gottlieb Fichte, *Erste Einleitung in die Wissenschaftslehre, Johann Gottlieb Fichte Werke: Auswahl in sechs Bänden*, vol. 3, ed. Fritz Medicus (Leipzig: Fritz Eckardt, 1910), p. 431.

78. Schleiermacher, *Drittes Tagebuch*, "Denkmale," p. 69.

79. I will not analyze Schleiermacher's relationship to Schelling. My decision is based on my agreement with Hermann Süskind, who, in his book *Der Einfluß Schellings auf die Entwicklung von Schleiermachers System* argues that Schleiermacher's basic idea of a theory of identity of the ideal and the real as a necessary component in any adequate theory of knowledge did not develop from Schleiermacher's study of Schelling. Rather, Schleiermacher's notion emerged parallel to Schelling's own concept of identity. Schleiermacher subsequently discovered this parallel in their thought and only then further developed his own ideas in a manner in keeping with Schelling's own notions (p. 97). In this work, I wish to explore the *roots* rather than *the subsequent development* of Schleiermacher's theory of the unity of the self.

80. Cited in Michael Ermarth's book, *Wilhelm Dilthey: The Critique of Historical Reason* (Chicago: The University of Chicago Press, 1978), p. 45.

81. Ibid.

82. Vleeschauwer, *The Development of Kantian Thought*, p. 111.

83. Ibid., p. 110.

84. Wolfgang Carl, "Kant's First Drafts of the Deductions of the Categories," *Kant's Transcendental Deductions*, p. 17.

85. Ibid., p. 3.

86. Ibid., p. 5.

87. Ibid., p. 20.

Chapter 2. Fichte's Insight

1. Johann Gottlieb Fichte, *Zweite Einleitung in die Wissenschaftslehre für Leser die schon ein philosophisches System haben, Johann Gottlieb Fichte Werke: Auswahl in sechs Bänden*, vol. 3, ed. Fritz Medicus (Leipzig: Fritz Eckardt, 1910), p. 501.

2. This letter was first brought to my attention in Albert L. Blackwell's book, *Schleiermacher's Early Philosophy of Life: Determinism, Freedom and Phantasy* (Chico, California: Scholars Press, 1982). The translation of this letter is by Terrence N. Tice. The letter was written on January 4, 1800, to Schleiermacher's friend C. G. von Brinkmann, and can be found in *Aus Schleiermacher's Leben in Briefe*, vol. 4, ed. Wilhelm Dilthey (Berlin: Georg Reimer, 1863), p. 53. Also of KGA III.5 (1992), eds. Andreas Arndt und Wolfgang Virmond, pp. 313–14.

3. Dilthey, *Leben Schleiermachers*, vol. 1, pp. 336–38.

4. Cited by Blackwell, p. 157. August 29, 1800. *Brief Friedrich Schleiermachers an August Wilhelm Schlegel*, p. 752.

5. Ibid. September 16, 1802. *Briefe*, I, p. 339.

6. Dieter Henrich, *Fichtes ursprüngliche Einsicht* (Frankfurt: Klostermann, 1967), pp. 15–16.

7. Ibid., p. 16.

8. Ibid., pp. 19–20.

9. It is important to note here that Fichte did not consider himself a Kantian but rather thought himself one who clearly understood and expounded the presuppositions upon which Kant based his work. (*Zweite Einleitung*, p. 481n.)

10. Johann Gottlieb Fichte, *Erste Einleitung in die Wissenschaftslehre, Johann Gottlieb Fichte Werke: Auswahl in sechs Bänden*, vol. 3, ed. Fritz Medicus (Leipzig: Fritz Eckardt, 1910) p. 455.

11. Zweig, from J. S. Beck, June 24, 1797, p. 232.

12. Fichte, *Erste Einleitung*, p. 455.

13. John H. Taber, *Transformative Philosophy: A Study of Sankara, Fichte, and Heidegger* (Honolulu: University of Hawaii Press, 1983), p. 69.

14. Ibid., pp. 2 and 128. Taber calls philosophic standpoints that expound such transformations, "transformative philosophy," and claims that such thinking is intelligible only to a gifted few (p. 3).

15. Henrich, "Fichte's Original Insight," p. 51.

16. Fichte, *Zweite Einleitung*, p. 479n.

17. Fichte believed that Kant, himself, had *conceived of* such a system, that all which he actually expounds are fragments and results of this system, and that Kant's statements only have meaning, coherence, and cohesion by means of this presupposition. Ibid., p. 478.

18. Reinhard Lauth, "Fichtes und Reinholds Verhältnis vom Anfange ihrer Bekanntschaft bis zu Reinholds Beitritt zum Stand-

punkt der Wissenschaftslehre Anfang 1797," *Philosophie aus einem Prinzip Karl Leonhard Reinhold*, ed. Reinhard Lauth, *Conscientia: Studien zur Bewußtseinsphilosophie*, Band 6, eds. Gerhard Funke et al. (Bonn: Bouvier Verlag Herbert Grundmann, 1974), p. 133.

19. Lauth, p. 133.

20. Johann Gottlieb Fichte, *Über den Begriff der Wissenschaftslehre oder der sogenannten Philosophie, Johann Gottlieb Fichte's Sämmtliche Werke*, vol. 1, ed. J. H. Fichte (Berlin: Veit und Comp., 1845).

21. Ibid., p. 138.

22. *Wissenschaftslehre*, I, pp. 95–100. Johann Gottlieb Fichte, *Grundlage der gesammten Wissenschaftslehre, Fichtes sämmtliche Werke*, vol. 1 (Berlin: Veit und Comp., 1845), pp. 98–100. Heidegger's own characterization of the implications of Fichte's claim is worth noting here. According to Heidegger, "The statement 'I = I' is more comprehensive than the formally general statement 'A = A'—a remarkable state of affairs. And we do not exaggerate when we claim that to this day we have not clarified what this matter touches upon, which for thinking means we have not found its originating character worthy of questioning." ("Principles of Thinking," *The Piety of Thinking: Essays by Martin Heidegger*, eds. James G. Hart and John C. Maraldo [Bloomington: Indiana University Press, 1976], p. 54.)

23. Johann Gottlieb Fichte, *Werke*, vol. 6, pp. 145–311.

24. Schleiermacher, "Fichtes Bestimmung," p. 528.

25. Ibid.

26. Ibid.

27. Wilhelm Dilthey, *Leben Schleiermachers*, vol. 1, (Berlin: Georg Reimer, 1870).

28. Ibid., p. 399.

29. Hermann Süskind, like Dilthey, also notes Fichte's positive legacy to Schleiermacher's *Dialektik*. Süskind, in his book *Der Einfluß Schellings auf die Entwicklung von Schleiermachers System* (neudruck der Ausgabe Tübingen 1909, Darmstadt: Scientia Verlag Aalen, 1983), p. 55, summarizes this influence by juxtaposing it to that which Schleiermacher adamantly rejected in Fichte's work. According to Süskind: "The reaction of Schleiermacher against Fichte consists, above all, in the two thoughts of individuality and of the constructing of an ethics. Concerning the positive reaction—a few further Fichtean thoughts by Schleiermacher about the latter, first coming to the fore in the *Dialektik*—is the idea of a theory of knowledge [*Wissenschaftslehre*]." Albert Blackwell, on the other hand, in his book *Schleiermacher's Early Philosophy of Life: Determinism, Freedom, and*

Phantasy, bases most of his examination of Fichte's influence on Schleiermacher's assessment of Fichte's *philosophy*, which as we have seen, was scathing. Blackwell does not investigate that which Fichte's philosophy presupposes, that is, the pure *I*, which for Fichte is the transcendental ground of his philosophy. Concerning this issue, Blackwell states, "Our interest here is not so much in Fichte's fundamental principle *per se* as in the claim he makes about the possibility of systematically deducing all philosophy, and indeed all experience, from it, completely *a priori* (p. 57)." As this present work seeks to demonstrate, such a focus by Blackwell is problematic, if an adequate assessment of Fichte's positive legacy to Schleiermacher is to be ascertained.

    30. Wilhelm Dilthey, *Leben Schleiermachers*, vol. 2, ed. Martin Redeker, *Wilhelm Dilthey's Gesammelte Schriften*, vol. 14 (Göttingen: Vandenhöck & Ruprecht, 1966), p. 71.

    31. Ibid., p. 72.

    32. Fichte, *Erste Einleitung*, p. 455.

    33. Zweig, pp. 213–15.

    34. Ibid., pp. 216–17.

    35. Jacob Sigismund Beck, *Erläuternder Auszug aus den critischen Schriften des herrn Prof. Kant auf Anrathen desselben: Einzig möglicher Standpunct aus welchem die critische Philosophie beurtheilt werden muss*, vol. 3 (Riga: Johan Friedrich Hartknoch, 1796), p. 12. I will refer to this volume as Beck's *Standpunct*.

    36. I must note here that I use the term *object* to translate both German words *Gegenstand* and *Object*. I use a lowercase *o* when translating *Gegenstand* and an uppercase *O* when translating *Object*. I make this distinction because of the critical difference in meaning between the two usages in Beck's work. For Beck, *Gegenstand* refers to objective consciousness, or that which is thought. *Object*, on the other hand, refers to that which is distinct from thought but to which thought must refer if it is to have meaning. *Object* in this way refers to that which *Gegenstand* presupposes. Both terms, however, refer to that which is within the self and not to something distinct from the self, that is, to a thing-in-itself.

    37. Ibid., p. 12.

    38. Ibid.

    39. Ibid.

    40. Ibid., p. 11.

    41. Ibid., p. 13.

    42. Ibid., p. 140.

    43. Ibid., p. 139.

44. Ibid., pp. 124–25.
45. Ibid., p. 125.
46. Ibid., p. 120.
47. Ibid., p. 124.
48. Ibid.
49. Ibid., p. 133.
50. Ibid., pp. 126–27.
51. Ibid.
52. Ibid., p. 483.
53. Ibid., p. 483n.
54. Ibid., p. 503.
55. Ibid., pp. 454–55.
56. Ibid., p. 485.
57. Fichte used the masculine pronoun to refer to the philosopher.
58. Fichte, *Zweite Einleitung*, p. 458.
59. Ibid. "Die erste Frage sonach wäre die: Wie ist das Ich für sich selbst?"
60. Ibid., p. 99.
61. Ibid., p. 478.
62. Ibid., p. 479. "Der Definition dieser Kategorien überhebe ich mich in dieser Abhandlung geflißentlich, ob ich fleich im Besitz derselben sein möchte."
63. Ibid., p. 479n.
64. Ibid., p. 508.
65. Ibid., p. 489.
66. Ibid.
67. Ibid., p. 492.
68. Ibid., p. 491.
69. Ibid., p. 462.
70. Ibid., p. 492. "Ich bestimme mir durch das Denken eines Entgegengesetzten meine Anschauung; dies und nichts anderes bedeutet der Ausdruck: ich begreife die Anschauung."
71. Ibid., p. 458.
72. Ibid.
73. Ibid.
74. Ibid.
75. Ibid., p. 463.
76. Ibid., p. 472. "Die intellektuelle Anschauung, von welcher die Wissenschaftslehre redet, geht gar nicht auf ein Sein, sondern auf ein Handeln, und sie ist bei Kant gar nicht bezeichnet (auser, wenn man will, durch den Ausdruck reine Apperzeption)."

77. Ibid., p. 461.

78. Ibid., p. 459. "Jenes sich selbst konstruierende Ich ist kein anderes, als sein eigenes."

79. Fichte, *A Comparison between Prof. Schmid's System and the Wissenschaftslehre* [Excerpt translated by Daniel Breazeale in *Fichte: Early Philosophical Writings*] (Ithaca: Cornell University Press, 1988), pp. 323–24, II, pp. 442–43.

80. Henrich, "Fichte's Original Insight," pp. 19–20.

81. Ibid., p. 21.

82. Ibid., p. 26.

83. Fichte, *Zweite Einleitung*, p. 463.

84. Ibid., p. 463.

85. Ibid., p. 530.

86. Ibid., pp. 466-67.

87. Ibid. Emphasis added.

88. Ibid., p. 530.

89. Friedrich Schleiermacher, "J. G. Fichte. Die Grundzüge des gegenwärtigen Zeitalters dargestellt in Vorlesungen, gehalten zu Berlin im Jahre 1804–1805," *Aus Schleiermacher's Leben*, vol. 4, comp. Ludwig Jonas, ed. Wilhelm Dilthey (Berlin: Georg Reimer, 1863), p. 626.

90. Ibid.

91. Ibid., p. 627.

92. Ibid., p. 626.

93. Ibid., pp. 629ff.

94. Kant, *Philosophical Correspondence, 1759–99*. Ed. and trans. by Arnulf Zweig. Chicago: The University of Chicago Press, 1967. (Henceforth referred to as Zweig.) Pp. 253–54.

95. Vleeschauwer, *The Development of Kantian Thought*, p. 160.

96. Ibid.

97. Ibid., pp. 159–60.

98. Wolfgang Carl, "Kant's First Drafts of the Deduction of the Categories," *Kant's Transcendental Deductions*, ed. Eckart Förster (Stanford: Stanford University Press, 1989), p. 5.

99. Vleeschauwer, *The Development of Kantian Thought*, p. 108.

100. Ibid., p. 113.

101. Ibid., p. 112.

102. Ibid.

103. Ibid.

104. Schleiermacher, "Fichtes Bestimmung," p. 528.

Chapter 3. Schleiermacher's New Vocabulary for Consciousness

1. The philosophic problem of sense perception in Western thought pertains to basic epistemological issues. As Roderick Firth notes in his essay "Sense Experience" in *Historical and Philosophical Roots of Perception*, Vol. 1 [eds. Edward C. Carterette and Morton P. Friedman (New York: Academic Press, 1974)], pp. 4–5: "The question 'What is *empirical* knowledge?'," which has dominated the history of modern philosophy, leads even more certainly to problems of perception. For if 'empirical knowledge' means knowledge based on some form of observation, then all empirical knowledge of the 'external world' is presumably based on perception. . . . In order to answer the question 'What is knowledge?' it is first necessary to answer the question 'What makes a belief warranted (or justified?)'. . . . And if all empirical knowledge is somehow based on perception, it becomes a matter of special importance for epistemology to know what makes a *perceptual* belief (or judgment) warranted. It is fair to say, I think, that this is what most philosophers have in mind when they speak of 'the problem of perception'."

2. In an 1814 lecture, he refers to this exterior Being as *Das äußere Sein* (D234).

3. "*Und als erste solche Affection ist nun anzusehen das (actio gedachte) Öffnen der Sinne als das Einströmen der Einwirkungen des Außenseins bedingend*" (D554n).

Chapter 4. Schleiermacher's Original Insight

1. W. B. Selbie, in his book *Schleiermacher: A Critical and Historical Study* (New York: E. P. Dutton & Co., 1913), p. 238, aptly characterizes Schleiermacher's fame as follows: "It is true that [Schleiermacher] founded no school in the strict sense of the term, but he was the originator of a new method and the embodiment of a new spirit. Every theologian of note who comes after him, is more or less in his debt, and with many of them the debt is greater than they will acknowledge. Even those who oppose him cannot help using him, and their imitation of him is sometimes more significant than their criticism. He overthrew once and for all the rationalist theory of 'natural' religion and the rationalist estimate of Christian theology. He vindicated the right of religion to be, and to be considered among the subjects of paramount human interest and importance."

2. For a specific use of the term *Modalität* see the following: "*Das Wissen sezt also voraus, daß dasselbige gesezt sein könne im*

Wahrnehmen wie im Denken, aber im Wahrnehmen auf eine andere Weise als im Denken, und daß, diese Differenz der Modalität abgerechtnet, die Totalität des Wahrnehmens gleich sei der Totalität des Denkens." (D396)

3. *"Die Grenze zwischen beiden, ein Aufgehörthaben des einen und Nochnicht-angefangenhaben des andern."*

4. Further: "Fragt man . . . Was heist das, ich seze bei meinem Denken dies voraus: so ist die Antwort, Nichts anderes, als ich handle in meinem Denken danach (D509n)." (If one asks: What does it mean to say that I presuppose this in my thinking? The answer is: Nothing other than that I act in accord with it in my thinking.")

5. Richard H. Popkin's book *The History of Scepticism from Erasmus to Descartes* (The Netherlands: Van Gorcum & Co., 1960) is an excellent introduction to the crisis. Popkin argues that the search for an adequate 'rule of faith' instigated by the Reformation's subjective basis for belief was coupled with Pyrrhonian skepticism that claimed that all judgments on all questions of knowledge should be suspended because there was insufficient and inadequate evidence to determine if any knowledge were possible. This convergence led to the *crise pyrrhonienne* of the early seventeenth century and Descartes's heroic but failed attempt to slay this skeptical specter. Schleiermacher, like Kant, is heir to this formidable task.

6. *"Die ganze Behauptung beruht auf dem Saz, das die Gesammtheit des uns gegebenen Seins mit dem in der Intelligenz liegenden System von Begriffen identisch sei."* ("The entire claim rests on the presupposition that the totality of being given to us is identical with the system of concepts lying in our intellect.")

7. William James, *The Varieties of Religious Experience: A Study in Human Nature* (New York: Penguin Books, 1982), pp. 387–88.

8. Ibid., p. 388.

9. Referring respectively to the ethical and physical forms of thinking, Schleiermacher states: "Offenbar hat nun diese Entgegensezung dem Verhaltnis des Denkens zum Sein im *vorbildlichen und abbildlichen* Denken ihren eigentlichen Ort in derjenigen Reihe unseres Bewußtseins, wo der Wechsel zwischen beiden vorkommt und das Selbstbewußtsein in der Identitat desselben sich geltend machen."

10. Saint Teresa, cited in William James, *The Varieties of Religious Experience*, p. 411n. Cited from Bartoli-Michel's *Vie de Saint Ignace de Loyola*, i, pp. 581 and 582.

11. Henrich, "Fichte's ursprüngliches Einsicht," p. 32; ET: "Fichte's Original Insight," p. 36.

12. Ibid.

13. I am grateful to Dean Ronald F. Thiemann for making this suggestion to me after I read a paper based on this present study at Harvard Divinity School on October 8, 1992.

14. Alfred North Whitehead, *Science and the Modern World* (New York: The Free Press, 1967).

15. Ibid., pp. 58–59.

16. Hans-Richard Reuter, *Die Einheit der Dialektik Friedrich Schleiermachers: Eine systematische Interpretation* (München: Chr. Kaiser Verlag, 1979).

17. Ibid., p. 240.

18. Ibid., p. 245.

19. Ibid., p. 240. "... *die dialektische reduction ad hominem gibt zu verstehen, sie sei eine Reduktion des Menschen auf seine ursprüngliche Menschlichkeit.*"

20. "Unser Wissen um das Wissen ist vielmehr die Reflexion auf daß als Überzeugung begleitende Selbstbewußtsein" (D539).

Chapter 5. The Embodied Self

1. G. W. F. Hegel, *Faith & Knowledge*, trans. Walter Cerf and H. S. Harris (Albany: State University of New York Press, 1977), p. 154.

2. Ibid., pp. 64–65.

3. Hegel, "Über die Reflexionsphilosphie der Subjectivität," *Journal für Philosophie*, vol. 2, cited by Dilthey in *Leben Schleiermachers*, vol. 1, p. 338n.

4. G. W. F. Hegel, *The Difference between Fichte's and Schelling's System of Philosophy*, trans. H. S. Harris and Walter Cerf (Albany: State University of New York Press, 1977), p. 173.

5. Ibid.

6. Ibid., p. 81.

7. G. W. F. Hegel, *Hegel's Science of Logic*, trans. A.V. Miller (Atlantic Highlands, NJ: Humanities Press International, Inc., 1969), pp. 42–78.

8. Ibid., p. 77.

9. Ibid., p. 56.

10. Ibid., p. 69.

11. Ibid., p. 48.

12. Ibid., p. 50.

13. Alexandre Kojève, *Introduction to the Reading of Hegel: Lectures on the Phenomenology of Spirit*, ed. Allan Bloom, trans. James H. Nichols, Jr. (Ithaca: Cornell University Press, 1969), p. 147.

14. Hegel, *Faith & Knowledge*, p. 65.

15. Ibid., p. 147.
16. Ibid., p. 147n.
17. Richard Crouter, "Hegel and Schleiermacher at Berlin: A Many-Sided Debate," *Journal of the American Academy of Religion* (1980), p. 37.
18. Ibid.

Selected Bibliography

Barth, Ulrich. *Christentum und Selbstbewußtsein*, Göttingen: Vanden-höck & Ruprecht, 1983.

Beck, Jacob Sigismund. *Erläuternder Auszug aus den critischen Schriften des herrn Prof. Kant auf Anrathen desselben: Einzig möglicher Standpunct aus welchem die critische Philosophie beurtheilt werden muß*, vol. 3. Riga: Johann Friedrich Hartknoch, 1796.

Blackwell, Albert L. *Schleiermacher's Early Philosophy of Life: Determininism, Freedom and Phantasy*, Harvard Theological Studies. Chico, California: Scholars Press, 1982.

Brandt, Richard B. *The Philosophy of Schleiermacher: The Development of His Theory of Scientific and Religious Knowledge*. New York: Harper & Brothers, 1941.

Crouter, Richard. "Hegel and Schleiermacher at Berlin: A Many-Sided Debate," *Journal of the American Academy of Religion*. 1980.

de Vleeschauwer, Herman-J. *La Déduction Transcendentale dans L'Oeuvre de Kant*. Paris: Librairie Ernest Leroux, 1934–1937.

———. *The Development of Kantian Thought: History of a Doctrine*, trans. A. R. C. Duncan. Toronto: Thomas Nelson and Sons Ltd., 1962.

Dilthey, Wilhelm, ed. *Aus Schleiermachers Leben*, vol. 4, comp. Ludwig Jonas. Berlin: Georg Reimer, 1863.

———. *Die Jugendgeschichte Hegels und Andere Abhandlungen zur Geschichte des Deutschen Idealismus*, *Wilhelm Dilthey's Gesammelte Schriften*, vol. 4. Leipzig: B. G. Teubner, 1921.

———. *Leben Schleiermachers*, vol. 1, Berlin: Georg Reimer, 1870.

———. *Leben Schleiermachers*, vol. 2, ed. Martin Redeker. *Wilhelm Dilthey's Gesammelte Schriften*, vol. 14. Göttingen: Vandenhoeck & Ruprecht, 1966.

Ermarth, Michael. *Wilhelm Dilthey: The Critique of Historical Reason*, Chicago: The University of Chicago Press, 1978.

Fackenheim, Emil L. "Immanuel Kant," *Nineteenth Century Religious Thought in the West*, eds. Ninian Smart, John Clayton, Patrick Sherry, and Steven T. Katz. Cambridge: Cambridge University Press, 1985.

Fichte, Johann Gottlieb. *A Comparison between Prof. Schmid's System and the Wissenschaftslehre* [Excerpt translated by Daniel Breazeale in *Fichte: Early Philosophical Writings*]. Ithaca: Cornell University Press, 1988.

———. *Erste Einleitung in die Wissenschaftslehre, Johann Gottlieb Fichte Werke: Auswahl in sechs Bänden*, vol. 3, ed. Fritz Medicus. Leipzig: Fritz Eckardt, 1910.

———. *Fichte: Science of Knowledge (Wissenschaftslehre) with First and Second Introductions*, eds. and trans. Peter Heath and John Lachs. New York: Appleton-Century-Crofts, 1970.

———. *Grundlage der gesammten Wissenschaftslehre, Fichte's sämmtliche Werke*, vol. 1. Berlin: Veit and Comp., 1845.

———. *Über den Begriff der Wissenschaftslehre oder der sogenannten Philosophie, Johann Gottlieb Fichte's sämmtliche Werke*, vol. 1, ed. J. H. Fichte. Berlin: Veit und Comp., 1845.

———. *Versuch einer neuen Darstellung der Wissenschaftslehre, Fichtes sämmtliche Werke*, vol. 1, ed. J. H. Fichte. Berlin: Veit and Comp., 1845.

———. *Zweite Einleitung in die Wissenschaftslehre für Leser, die schon ein philosophisches System haben, Johann Gottlieb Fichte Werke: Auswahl in sechs Bänden*, vol. 3, ed. Fritz Medicus. Leipzig: Fritz Eckardt, 1910.

Firth, Roderick. "Sense Experience," *Historical and Philosophical Roots of Perception*, vol. 1, eds. Edward C. Carterette and Morton P. Friedman, New York: Academic Press, 1974.

Förster, Eckart. "Is there a 'Gap' in Kant's Critical System?" *Journal of the History of Philosophy*, 25:4 (October 1987).

———, ed. *Kant's Transcendental Deductions.* Stanford: Stanford University Press, 1989.

Forstman, Jack. *A Romantic Triangle: Schleiermacher and Early German Romanticism*. Missoula, Montana: Scholars Press, 1977.

Frank, Manfred. *Das individuelle Allgemeine: Textstrukturierung und –interpretation nach Schleiermacher*. Frankfurt a.M.: Suhrkamp, 1985.

Green, Ronald M. *Kierkegaard and Kant: The Hidden Debt*. Albany: State University of New York Press, 1992.

Harris, William. "Preface," *The Science of Knowledge*, J. G. Fichte, trans. A. E. Kroeger. London: Truebner & Co., Ludgate Hill, 1889.

Hart, James G. and John C. Maraldo. *The Piety of Thinking: Essays by Martin Heidegger*. Bloomington: Indiana University Press, 1976.

Hartshorne, Charles and William L. Reese. *Philosophers Speak of God*. Chicago: The University of Chicago Press, 1953; reprint, Chicago: Midway Reprint, 1976.

Hegel, G. W. F. *The Difference Between Fichte's and Schelling's System of Philosophy*, trans. by H. S. Harris and Walter Cerf. Albany: State University of New York Press, 1977.

———. *Faith & Knowledge*, trans. by Walter Cerf and H. S. Harris. Albany: State University of New York Press, 1977.

———. *Hegel's Science of Logic*, trans. A. V. Miller. Atlantic Highlands, NJ: Humanities Press International, Inc., 1969.

Henrich, Dieter. *Fichtes ursprüngliche Einsicht*. Frankfurt: Klostermann, 1967. English translation by David R. Lachterman, "Fichte's Original Insight," *Contemporary German Philosophy I*. University Park: Pennsylvania State University Press, 1982.

Hirsch, Emanuel. *Geschichte der Neuern Evangelischen Theologie*. Gütersloh: C. Bertelsmann Verlag, 1949.

James, William. *The Varieties of Religious Experience: A Study in Human Nature*. New York: Penguin Books, 1982.

Kant, Immanuel. *Immanuel Kant's Critique of Pure Reason*, unabridged ed., trans. Norman Kemp Smith. New York: Macmillan & Co., 1929; New York: St. Martin's Press, 1965.

Kojève, Alexandre. *Introduction to the Reading of Hegel: Lectures on the Phenomenology of Spirit*, trans. J. H. Nicholas. Ithaca: Cornell University Press, 1969.

Lauth, Reinhard. "Fichtes und Reinholds Verhältnis vom Anfange ihrer Bekanntschaft bis zu Reinholds Beitritt zum Standpunkt der Wissenschaftslehre Anfang 1797," *Philosophie aus einem Prinzip Karl Leonhard Reinhold*, ed. Reinhard Lauth. *Conscientia: Studien zur Bewußtseinsphilosophie*, vol. 6. Bonn: Bouvier Verlag Herbert Grundmann, 1974.

Mann, Gustav. *Das Verhältnis der Scheiermacher'schen Dialektik zur Schelling'schen Philosophie, Inaugural-Dissertation zur Langung der Doktorwuerde der Philosophischen Fakultät (I. Sektion) der K. Ludwig-Maximillians-Universität zu München.* Stuttgart: Druck der Stuttgarter, 1941.

Mehl, Paul Frederick. *Schleiermacher's Mature Doctrine of God as Found in the Dialektik of 1822 and the Second Edition of the Christian Faith (1830–31).* Columbia University, 1961.

Michalson, Gordon E., Jr. *Fallen freedom: Kant on radical evil and moral regeneration.* Cambridge: Cambridge University Press, 1990.

Odebrecht, Rudolf. "Das Gefüge des religiösen Bewußtseins bei Fr. Schleiermacher," *Blätter für Deutsche Philosophie.* 1934–35.

Popkin, H. Richard. *The History of Scepticism from Erasmus to Descartes.* Assen: Van Gorcum & Comp., 1960.

Redeker, Martin. *Schleiermacher: Life and Thought,* trans. John Wallhausser. Philadelphia: Fortress Press, 1973.

Reinhold, Karl Leonhard. *Briefe über die Kantische Philosophie,* vol. 1. Leipzig: Georg Joachim Goschen, 1790–1792.

———. *Über das Fundament des philosophischen Wissens.* Jena: Johann Michael Mauke, 1791.

Reuter, Hans-Richard. *Die Einheit der Dialektik Friedrich Schleiermachers: Eine systematische Interpretation.* München: Chr. Kiser Verlag, 1979.

Scharlemann, Robert P., ed. *Theology at the End of the Century: A Dialogue on the Postmodern.* Charlottesville: University Press of Virginia, 1990.

Schleiermacher, Friedrich. *Anthropologie von Immanuel Kant, Aus Schleiermachers Leben,* vol. 4, ed. Wilhelm Dilthey. Berlin: Georg Reimer, 1863.

———. *Christian Faith,* English Translation of the Second German Edition, eds. H. R. Mackintosh and J. S. Stewart. Philadelphia: Fortress Press, 1976.

———. *Dialektik,* aus Schleiermachers Handschriftlichem Nachlasse, ed. Ludwig Jonas. *Friedrich Schleiermacher's sämmtliche Werke,* III, 4, 2. Berlin: Georg Reimer, 1839.

———. *Drittes Tagebuch, Lebens Schleiermacher,* vol. 1, ed. Wilhelm Dilthey. Berlin: Georg Reimer, 1870.

———. *Erstes Tagebuch, Lebens Schleiermacher,* vol. 1, ed. Wilhelm Dilthey. Berlin: Georg Reimer, 1870.

———. *Fichtes Bestimmung des Menschen, Schleiermachers sämmtliche Werke,* III, 1. Berlin: Georg Reimer, 1839.

――――. *Friedrich Schleiermacher Kritische Gesamtausgabe Schriften und Entwurfe*, I. 1. *Jugendschriften 1787–1796*. ed. Gunter Meckenstock. Berlin: Walter de Gruyter, 1984.

――――. *Friedrich Schleiermacher Kritische Gesamtausgabe Schriften und Entwurfe*, III.1. *Schriften aus der Berliner Zeit 1800–1802*. ed. Gunter Meckenstock. Berlin: Walter de Gruyter, 1988.

――――. *Friedrich Schleiermacher Kritische Gesamtausgabe Briefwechsel 1799–1800*, III.5. eds Andreas Arndt and Wolfgang Virmond. Berlin: Walter de Gruyter, 1992.

――――. *F. W. J. Schelling: Vorlesungen über die Methode des akademischen Studiums, Aus Schleiermachers Leben*, vol. 4, ed. Wilhelm Dilthey. Berlin: Georg Reimer, 1863.

――――. *Grundlinien einer Kritik der bisherigen Sittenlehre, Friedrich Schleiermachers sämmtliche Werke*, III, 1. Berlin: Georg Reimer, 1846.

――――. *On Religion: Addresses in Response to its Cultured Critics*, trans. Terrence N. Tice. Richmond, Virginia: John Knox Press, 1969.

――――. *On Religion: Speeches to its Cultured Despisers*, trans. Richard Crouter. Cambridge: Cambridge University Press, 1988.

――――. *On the Glaubenslehre: Two Letters to Dr. Luke*, trans. James Duke and Francis Fiorenza. Chico: Scholars Press, 1981.

――――. *Schleiermacher's Introduction to Plato's Dialogues*, trans. William Dobson. New York: Arno Press, 1973.

――――. *Über die Religion: Reden an die Gebildeten unter ihren Verächtern*. Hamburg: Fexlis Meiner, 1958.

Selbie, W. B. *Schleiermacher: A Critical and Historical Study*. New York: E. P. Dutton & Co., 1913.

Spiegler, Gerhard. *Schleiermacher's Experiment in Cultural Theology: The Eternal Covenant*. New York: Harper & Row, 1967.

Süskind, Hermann. *Der Einfluß Schellings auf die Entwicklung von Schleiermachers System*, neudruck der Ausgabe Tübingen 1909. Darmstadt: Scientia Verlag Aalen, 1983.

Taber, John A. *Transformative Philosophy: A Study of Sankara, Fichte, and Heidegger*. Honolulu: University of Hawaii Press, 1983.

Taylor, Mark C. *Erring: A Postmodern A/theology*. Chicago: The University of Chicago Press, 1984.

Thiel, John E. *God and World in Schleiermacher's Dialektik and Glaubenslehre: Criticism and the Methodology of Dogmatics. Basler und Berner Studien zur historischen und systematischen Theologie*, vol 43. Bern: Peter Lang, 1981.

————. *Imagination and Authority: Theological Authorship in the Modern Tradition.* Minneapolis: Fortress Press, 1991.

Watson, Richard. *The Downfall of Cartesianism, 1673–1712.* The Hague: Martinus Nijhoff, 1966.

Wehrung, Georg. *Der geschichtesphilosophische Standpunkt Schleiermachers zur Zeit seiner Freundschaft mit den Romantikern: Zugleich ein Beitrag zur Entwicklungsgeschichte Schleiermachers in den Jahren 1787–1800.* Stuttgart: Fr. Frommanns Verlag (E. Hauff), 1907.

Whitehead, Alfred North. *Process and Reality*, corrected edition, eds. David Ray Griffin and Donald W. Sherburne. New York: The Free Press, 1978.

Index